NO BAD DAYS

ADAPTED FOR YOUNG ADULTS

NO BAD DAYS

TURNING YOUR BIGGEST CHALLENGES
INTO YOUR GREATEST OPPORTUNITIES

JT MESTDAGH

Forefront
BOOKS

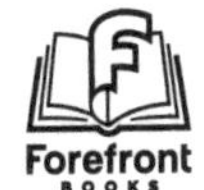

No Bad Days: Turning Your Biggest Challenges into Your Greatest Opportunities (Adapted for Young Adults)

Published by Forefront Books, Nashville, Tennessee.
Distributed by Simon & Schuster.

Library of Congress Control Number: 2024927212

Print ISBN: 978-1-63763-281-9
E-book ISBN: 978-1-63763-282-6

Cover Design by Bruce Gore, Gore Studio, Inc.
Interior Design by Bill Kersey, KerseyGraphics

Printed in the United States of America

TO MY AWESOME PARENTS,

who've always had my back, teaching me to bounce back when things go south, to have faith in myself even when it feels like nobody else does, to go all out and chase my dreams, to smash my goals, and, you know what's really cool? To spread kindness wherever I go.

CONTENTS

Introduction 9
chapter 1: Pole, Pole 15
chapter 2: Share Your Story 25
chapter 3: Pray for Someone 39
chapter 4: Inspire Others 49
chapter 5: Be a Friend 57
chapter 6: Create Memories 69
chapter 7: Take Off Your Mask 81
chapter 8: Pull Off the Label 95
chapter 9: Stretch Yourself 111
chapter 10: Walk in Somebody Else's Shoes 127
chapter 11: Get Some Green Time 143
chapter 12: Learn to Fall 159
chapter 13: Find Your Wolf Pack 175
chapter 14: Leave a Legacy 187
chapter 15: Keep Climbing 199
chapter 16: Stay Resilient 211
Acknowledgments 223
Notes 225
About the Author 229
Mission 231
Journal Prompts for *No Bad Days* 233

INTRODUCTION

HAVE YOU EVER FOUND YOURSELF IN A COUNTRY where they speak another language, eager to unwind with your favorite Netflix shows, only to be met with frustration as the characters from *Stranger Things* and *Outer Banks* are conversing in the local language? While you're relaxing near the beach in Mexico, Will, Dustin, Mike, Max, and Eleven are speaking to each other in Spanish, or as you're touring the canals of Venice, Sarah, John B, and JJ are speaking Italian.

Sure, you could rely on closed captioning and read the words at the bottom of the screen, even though it's a bit annoying. Now imagine that the actors and actresses are speaking in an unfamiliar language—and you can't read the subtitles!

For some of the estimated 43.5 million Americans who have some form of dyslexia, seemingly simple tasks like reading, writing, and speaking might seem impossible. They struggle to learn letters and sounds. They can't memorize numbers and facts. They process words and sentences too slowly to comprehend what they just read. Reading novels, magazine articles, and long books might seem as difficult as trying to ascend Mount Kilimanjaro, and subjects like math, chemistry, and foreign languages present entirely different challenges.

Trust me, I know exactly how they feel.

On October 8, 2018, after a grueling four-day climb, I reached the snow-capped peak of Mt. Kilimanjaro. Roughly twenty-five thousand people attempt to climb Mt. Kilimanjaro every year, and about one-third of them turn back because of altitude sickness, injury, or poor weather. Each year, rescuers evacuate approximately one thousand climbers from Mt. Kilimanjaro, and six or seven people (maybe more) die from high-altitude illness, falling, or other trauma.

Reaching Mt. Kilimanjaro's majestic summit was an accomplishment that changed my life forever. I conquered not only one of the world's most formidable physical peaks but also my inner mountains of doubt.

As demanding as climbing Mt. Kilimanjaro might have been, for me it was nothing compared to learning to read. I'm among those estimated 43.5 million Americans who are dyslexic. I also have short-term memory loss, making my condition worse. You can't reverse dyslexia. It's a lifelong condition that can be treated with tutoring, therapy, and teaching methods. With early identification and the proper help, most people with dyslexia eventually learn to read and write. It's a long, slow struggle—and it was especially hard for me.

In addition to my learning differences, I faced many physical problems as a child. I weighed 5 pounds, 2 ounces when I was born in Detroit, Michigan, on September 13, 1995. When I came out of my mother's womb, my skin and lips were blue. My mother heard someone say, "Cut the cord!" Nurses took me to the neonatal intensive care unit. My parents, Kristine and James Mestdagh, had to wait a week to hold me for the first time.

Reaching Mt. Kilimanjaro's majestic summit was an accomplishment that changed my life forever.

My parents didn't change diapers during the first year of my life. They changed a colostomy bag. See, the day after I was born, Dr. Frederick E. Rector used a tiny pair of surgical scissors to save my life for the first of many times. During a five-hour surgery, Dr. Rector corrected a condition that was blocking oxygen to my lungs and food to my stomach and created a colostomy bag because my digestive system wasn't formed properly.

Eventually, doctors diagnosed me with VATER syndrome, a combination of several birth defects that often happen in conjunction with one another. VATER stands for vertebrae, anus, trachea, esophagus, and the renal system (or kidneys). Infants with at least three of these birth defects are diagnosed with VATER syndrome. I was lucky enough to have all five.

Over my first year of life, I was hospitalized for a bad urinary tract infection, two hernias in my groin area, asthma, and pneumonia. By the time I was three years old, I had spent 250 days in the hospital. During my first

There are no "bad" days, only hard days.

sixteen years on Earth, I endured sixteen major surgeries, two of which were to correct a tethered spinal cord that might have caused permanent paralysis. Surgeons deconstructed and reconstructed my abdomen; eighteen inches of my colon were removed.

As painful as some of those surgeries and recoveries were for me, nothing was as emotionally draining and frustrating as trying to learn to read and write. When

I was in the fifth grade, my parents were called to a meeting in which a psychologist told them that I'd be illiterate for the rest of my life. A few months later, one of the school administrators told me I would not be allowed to reenroll.

If I've learned anything in life, it's that God throws plenty of obstacles in our way to test us. Yes, a door was slammed in my face. But my parents refused to keep it closed. Over the next seven years, I would learn that God wants to open doors for us. We only must let go and allow God to have his way.

My parents' faith helped me to endure my early struggles. They taught me that circumstances in life can make you bitter or better, and I've always been a glass half-full kind of guy. Over time, I became stronger in my faith in God, which made me more confident and self-assured. I know God has a plan for my life. As I've told my dad so many times, there are no "bad" days, only hard days.

At the age of twenty-three, reaching Kilimanjaro's peak gave me the confidence and self-assurance that I could do anything I put my mind to. It taught me that no matter what challenge God decided to throw my way, I could accomplish my goals with slow, steady steps, patience, and resilience.

That day on that mountaintop, I learned that when we overcome an obstacle, we build amazing qualities like perseverance, stamina, grit, and accountability. No matter how difficult life might feel at times, it's always possible to reach the summit. I refuse to be defined by my limitations. Instead, I embrace the inherent strength inside me, using every obstacle as a stepping stone toward my goals. I hope you enjoy reading about my journey.

CHAPTER ONE

POLE, POLE

After I graduated from High Point University in High Point, North Carolina, on May 5, 2018, I decided it was time to tackle the most heart-stopping challenge on my growing bucket list. It wasn't parachuting out of an airplane, dancing with death in a shark cage at Australia's Great Barrier Reef, riding a massive wave on the Pipeline in Hawaii, or challenging Joey Chestnut to a hot-dog eating contest on the Fourth of July. (Nope—none of those are on my list, except skydiving, which I've already checked off). Believe it or not, what I wanted to do was even more dangerous than all of that.

Before I jumped into the real world and found a full-time job, I wanted to climb Mt. Kilimanjaro, the highest peak in Africa and the tallest single freestanding mountain in the world at 19,341 feet. How tall is Mt. Kilimanjaro?

Well, by comparison, the tallest building in the world is the Burj Khalifa, a skyscraper in Dubai, United Arab Emirates. That architectural wonder is about 2,717 feet, just over a half-mile tall, and has 160 stories. How would you like to climb those stairs to work every day? But get this: To match Mt. Kilimanjaro's height, you would have to stack about seven Burj Khalifa skyscrapers on top of each other. Or, let me put it this way: The Grand Canyon, on average, is about six thousand feet deep, so you'd have to walk up and down that natural wonder more than three times to reach Mt. Kilimanjaro's height.

Mt. Kilimanjaro is in Tanzania, on the eastern side of Africa, not far from the Ugandan border and the Indian Ocean. The locals call it Kili. In their native Swahili, *kilima* means "mountain" and *njaro* is translated to "white" or "shining." So, Kilimanjaro is often interpreted as "Shining Mountain" or "Mountain of Whiteness" because of its breathtaking snow-capped summit.

My friends and I decided that we were going to climb Mt. Kilimanjaro's highest point, Uhuru Peak, located on the outer crater rim of Kibo, the tallest peak.

Of course, I wasn't going to attempt to climb Mt. Kilimanjaro alone, and I wasn't going to do it without properly training and preparing. My good friend and mentor, Ladi Lettovsky, and his wife, Martina, were going to make the trek with me. I met Ladi when I was eight years old. He was a ski instructor at Beaver Creek Resort in Colorado, and I was one of his first clients when we vacationed there for the Christmas holiday. Even though Ladi is older than me, we became very good friends and have gone on so many adventures together. I've learned so much from him about skiing, hiking, ice climbing, mountain climbing, kayaking, mountain biking, and bobsledding.

Ladi has climbed some of the tallest peaks around the world, and he took on the tasks of planning our expedition. Before tackling Mt. Kilimanjaro, we spent months climbing mountains together in Colorado, adapting to high elevations—although not as high as Kili's—and preparing our bodies for the grueling test.

Finally, on October 2, 2018, I left home to conquer one of the biggest challenges in the world, both mentally and physically. Just getting to Tanzania was a test of its own. We flew from Denver to Miami—already wearing our hiking boots—then took an eight-hour red-eye flight to Heathrow Airport in London, followed by a nine-hour flight to Nairobi and a short flight to Kilimanjaro.

I felt a mix of respect and anticipation during the flights. The silhouette of the mountain I'd seen so many times in photographs and videos filled my dreams as I slept.

Finally, around 3 a.m. the next day, we made our way through customs and arrived at our hotel in the small village of Moshi. Since we had worked so hard in Colorado to acclimate our bodies to higher elevations, Ladi wanted us to make our way back up to higher elevation on the mountain right away. So, after only four hours of sleep, we met our guides and started our journey.

Our lead guide was Simon Mtuy, the founder and director of SENE: Summit Expeditions and Nomadic Experience. He had a wide smile and deep laugh, and I was drawn to him immediately. His assistant guide, Manase Lyimo, was very friendly too. Simon is a Chagga tribesman and had been involved in expeditions since he was fourteen. He initially worked as a porter, carrying climbers' equipment up and down the mountain. He became a licensed guide at twenty-one and has been to Kili's summit more than three hundred times. I'm not sure his Apple Watch can even keep up with those steps!

Simon is one of the world's most accomplished trail runners—he established a Guinness World Record for the fastest unsupported ascent/descent of Mt. Kilimanjaro in 2006. He went up and back down the mountain in only nine hours, twenty-one minutes. It's a good thing he knew how to tackle Kili quickly, because Ladi wanted us to do it in only four days. It typically takes climbers seven or eight days to climb and descend Kili.

That morning, we made our way up a winding dirt path, passing through small villages and coffee and banana plantations. This journey led us to the entrance gates of Mt. Kilimanjaro National Park. Witnessing the mountain for the first time was even more breathtaking than I had imagined. Kilimanjaro appears to be suspended in the mist amidst dark gray clouds. The snow-capped peak, according to ancient Chagga beliefs, signified that Kilimanjaro was the sacred seat of God. The spectacular rooftop of Africa left an indelible impression on me—a colossal spectacle of mystery, danger, and awe.

Simon introduced us to fifteen porters who were going to accompany us on the expedition. They were hard-working and diligent people, and a few of them only spoke Swahili. They shouldered all the equipment we would need: tents, water, food, and even a portable

Witnessing the mountain for the first time was even more breathtaking than I had imagined.

groover (toilet). A few of them would make multiple trips up and down the mountain to our base camp, making sure we had an adequate supply of water and food. My deep respect for them grew to be immense.

As if climbing Mt. Kilimanjaro wasn't difficult enough, Ladi decided we would make the least traveled and most difficult climb up Kili—the Umbwe route. It's the shortest and most direct passage up the mountain, but it's also the steepest and most dangerous. In fact, one of the Kili guide companies estimates that only 60 to 70 percent of the climbers who take the Umbwe route make it up and down compared to up to 90 percent success on other routes.

And get this: Ladi added another layer of danger, because we were going to start on Umbwe and then cut over to the Western Breach. Here's what a guide company had to say about that route: "A Kilimanjaro ascent via the Western Breach route is the most challenging and also by far the most dangerous way to scale Kibo and reach Uhuru Peak. The danger lies not in the climb itself. It lies in the melting glaciers above the route. As the glaciers retreat they release previously bound up rocks."[1]

Back in January 2006, a group of Americans were climbing the Western Breach when a rockslide traveling at more than 125 feet per second killed three of them. Another climber and four porters were badly injured. Kibo's receding ice was believed to be the cause of the rockslide, and the incident became known as the Western Breach Tragedy.

I was happy that Ladi had confidence in me to handle the daunting challenge. I'm not going to lie: I knew it was going to be difficult and dangerous. On the first day of our ascent, we covered nearly seven miles, elevating ourselves from 5,382 feet to 9,356 feet above sea level. Negotiating a muddy path, we journeyed through a natural rainforest where encounters with black-and-white colobuses and blue monkeys added a unique dimension to the walk. We crossed paths with only one other hiker—a lone woman. We were surrounded by the glory of Mother Nature and not much else. But Simon made sure to encourage us to move slowly and appreciate our surroundings and God's beauty the entire way. The beginning of the trek presented challenges, with steep sections requiring us to use tree roots as makeshift steps and ladders. As we progressed, the trail narrowed and became much steeper, taking us along a ridge between the Lonzo River and Umbwe River. Towering trees surrounded us, and I had to use my hiking poles most of the time. When we reached Umbwe Cave Camp, we called it a day.

Pole, pole—pronounced "po-lay, po-lay"—means "slowly, slowly" in Swahili. For the porters and guides who have ascended and descended Kili so many times, it means so much more than that. Quite simply, it means that less is more. By taking fewer, slower steps, you will get to the top and do it faster. If you try to sprint to the summit, you'll undoubtedly be injured, suffer altitude sickness, or worse. By conserving our energy, we ensured that we would have plenty of stamina and strength to complete our mission.

As Simon says on his company's website, "*Pole pole* is also the way of life in Tanzania ('no hurry in Africa!') as people understand the value of taking life slowly, savoring the moment, the people, and the place where you are here and now."[2] It's so different from how we live in the United States. We're constantly moving, typing on our phones, scanning social media, or searching the Internet. We're connected to others through a virtual community but not much more. I'm pretty sure the Africans have figured out how to get the most from life.

Our second day of climbing wasn't as long as the first, but it wasn't any easier. The trail was much steeper and more difficult. Ladi went ahead of me, so I spent much of the day walking with Martina. We entered the climate zone

I felt as if God had painted the sky only for me.

known as the heath or moorland. The surreal landscape, shrouded in mist, consisted of rugged, rocky outcrops and vast, open expanses. I felt like we were in another world. Moss covered many of the trees and hung over the trail like spider webs.

During the second day, we spotted Mount Meru, forty miles away, in a sea of thick clouds. It's the second highest peak in Tanzania. After we passed through the exposed Umbwe Ridge, a moment of absolute awe arrived as we finally saw Kilimanjaro in the distance, rising through clouds in shades of blue and white. Kili was unlike anything I'd ever seen. We hiked almost four miles, rising to 13,020 feet. I felt so close to God up there. The majestic sunset of orange, red, and yellows was unlike any I'd ever seen. I was so at peace as the sun dropped below the clouds. I felt as if God had painted the sky only for me.

While waiting for dinner, Ladi climbed onto a rock and was able to get one bar of service on his cell phone. We called my parents together to tell them about our adventures the first two days. We wanted them to know we were safe.

At the break of dawn the next morning, our guides woke me up to assess my vitals, establishing a baseline of my breathing rate and oxygen saturation. Two days earlier, when we started our ascent, my breaths had numbered sixteen per minute. As we climbed higher, the count increased to twenty, thirty, and eventually forty. I was warned that when we reached the summit, I would probably be sucking oxygen at fifty breaths a minute! It would feel like I'd just sprinted a mile. Using an instrument called a pulse oximeter clipped on the end of my finger, the guides monitored the oxygen saturation in my blood. Normal rates are 95 to 100 percent. Mine was 84 percent.

The only time I'd climbed this high before, I'd suffered altitude sickness, which brings on headaches, dizziness, vomiting, fatigue, and worse. It was an awful experience, and I was determined not to let it happen again.

Martina asked me how I was feeling. She worked as a registered nurse in Colorado, so I knew I was in good hands. She and Ladi had established three levels of conditions for me. Level One was, "Yes, JT is good." Level Two was, "I don't feel so great." Level Three was, "Help!" As we ate breakfast and prepared to turn west and climb another 1,500 feet on our way to Kili's summit, we couldn't have known that it wouldn't be long before I would find myself crashing into Level Three, putting the entire expedition at risk.

CHAPTER TWO

SHARE YOUR STORY

BEFORE I SHARE THE HARROWING DETAILS OF MY last day on Mt. Kilimanjaro, I want to take you back to where it all started for me—in a birthing room at St. John Hospital and Medical Center in Detroit on September 13, 1995.

My parents, Jim and Kristine Mestdagh, had been married for four years when I was born. I was and still am an only child. I was born three weeks early, and my mom's pregnancy had gone well. They didn't have any reason to believe that there would be something wrong with me.

But when I came into the world, my skin and lips looked blue. It was a visible warning sign that my tissues and organs weren't receiving enough oxygen. Doctors and nurses immediately started treating me, and then they whisked me away to the neonatal intensive care unit. Mom and Dad never even got to hold me.

After a scary and long day, my parents were worried and exhausted. Mom was in quite a bit of pain and needed rest. After talking with the doctors, Dad decided to go home to get some sleep. He still didn't know the full extent of my health issues, but he was becoming more and more concerned.

Before Dad went to bed that night, he silently prayed, asking God for reassurance that I was going to be okay.

Let the little children come to me, and do not hinder them.

He pulled his Bible from the nightstand and opened it. The pages fell to the tenth chapter of the Gospel of Mark:

> People were bringing little children to Jesus for him to place his hands on them, but the disciples rebuked them. When Jesus saw this, he was indignant. He said to them, "Let the little children come to me, and do not hinder them, for the

> kingdom of God belongs to such as these. Truly I tell you, anyone who will not receive the kingdom of God like a little child will never enter it." And he took the children in his arms, placed his hands on them and blessed them. (Mark 10:13–16)

At that very moment, those were the exact words Dad needed to read. All these years later, Dad is still convinced that God's hands opened his Bible to that passage. He knew God was speaking to him, letting him know that He would take me in His arms, place His hands on me, and bless me. Dad felt comforted and reassured.

The next day, my parents heard the full rundown of my health problems.

Doctors told Mom and Dad that they needed to do emergency surgery to fix my trachea and esophagus and to disconnect my colon from my rectum and give me a colostomy. They would re-route my colon to two stomas, or openings, in my stomach wall. It was a very risky procedure for an infant who wasn't yet a day old. Yet, it was also my only chance at survival.

On September 14, 1995, Dr. Frederick E. Rector performed a nearly five-hour surgery to save my life. With his God-given talent and wisdom, Dr. Rector cleared my windpipe, reconnected my esophagus to my stomach, and inserted a colostomy to help me use the restroom. Dr. Rector saved my life, but my parents and I still faced a very long road to recovery and health.

Fifteen days after I was born, I was finally able to go home. Before we left, a nurse gave my parents a single sheet of paper. It was a copy of a short essay entitled "Welcome to Holland." There were eleven paragraphs and fewer than four hundred words that looked like they were typed on an old typewriter. The words were faded, as if the essay had been photocopied millions of times for the many parents who had given birth to a child with physical differences. The essay said:

> I am often asked to describe the experience of raising a child with a disability—to try to help people who have not shared that unique experience to understand it, to imagine how it would feel. It's like this . . .

When you're going to have a baby, it's like planning a fabulous vacation trip—to Italy. You buy a bunch of guidebooks and make your wonderful plans. The Coliseum. Michelangelo's *David*. The gondolas in Venice. You may learn some handy phrases in Italian. It's all very exciting.

After months of eager anticipation, the day finally arrives. You pack your bags and off you go. Several hours later, the plane lands. The stewardess comes in and says, "Welcome to Holland."

"Holland?!?" you say. "What do you mean Holland? I signed up for Italy! I'm supposed to be in Italy. All my life I've dreamed of going to Italy."

But there's been a change in the flight plan. They've landed in Holland and there you must stay.

The important thing is that they haven't taken you to a horrible, disgusting, filthy place, full of pestilence, famine, and disease. It's just a different place.

So you must go out and buy new guidebooks. And you must learn a whole new language. And you will meet a whole new group of people you would never have met.

It's just a different place. It's slower-paced than Italy, less flashy than Italy. But after you've been there for a while and you catch your breath, you look around . . . and you begin to notice that Holland has windmills . . . and Holland has tulips. Holland even has Rembrandts.

But everyone you know is busy coming and going from Italy . . . and they're all bragging about what a wonderful time they had there. And for the rest of your life, you will say, "Yes, that's where I was supposed to go. That's what I had planned."

And the pain of that will never, ever, ever, ever go away . . . because the loss of that dream is a very, very significant loss.

But . . . if you spend your life mourning the fact that you didn't get to Italy, you may never be free to enjoy the very special, the very lovely things . . . about Holland.[3]

Emily Perl Kingsley was an award-winning writer for *Sesame Street* for forty-five years until her retirement in 2015. She wrote the "Welcome to Holland" essay in 1987. Fourteen years earlier, Emily and her husband, Charles, gave birth to their son Jason, who was born with Down syndrome. Down syndrome is a genetic disorder that affects about one in every seven hundred babies in the US every year, according to the National Down Syndrome Society.

While Emily Kingsley and her husband might have ended up in Holland, instead of Italy like they were planning, Jason's birth was no mistake. His parents might not have planned for a baby born with Down syndrome, just like my parents hadn't prepared for a son born with so many health problems, but I know in my heart and soul that God was not at all surprised by our births.

God chose my parents for me, and He chose me for them. We are God's gifts to our parents, and our parents are His gifts to us. I believe that God had a plan and purpose for people like Jason and me—and our parents. A doctor told Jason's mother that he wouldn't be able to walk, talk, or learn. In fact, the doctor said he should be institutionalized, which is what society did with a lot of children with Down syndrome and other developmental differences back then.

Fortunately, Emily and Charles didn't listen to the doctor's advice. Emily became Jason's biggest supporter and was determined to provide him with a life of happiness, independence, and fulfillment. Emily became a vocal advocate for people born with Down syndrome and other differences. She cast people with differences on *Sesame Street,* including Tarah Schaeffer, an actress who uses a wheelchair. Jason appeared on *Sesame Street* for the first time when he was fifteen months old. He graduated from high school, attended college, and became an actor.

We are God's gifts to our parents, and our parents are His gifts to us.

In an interview in 2019, Emily said she wrote the "Welcome to Holland" essay after talking to a mother who had just had a baby with Down syndrome.

"I found myself telling her what it was like and out came this spontaneous analogy… 'Welcome to Holland,'" Emily said. "When I got home later I thought about it and realized that she had responded to our conversation and it had a positive impact on the new mom and it worked for her, made her feel a little better. I said to myself, 'That's not bad. I ought to write that down.' I did and mentioned it again to another new family a couple of weeks later. Shortly after that I was writing my CBS Movie-of-the-Week *Kids Like These* and decided to use it as the concluding scene of the movie. After that it sort of 'went viral,' as they say, and the rest is history. It just took off."[4]

Reading Emily's essay had a profound impact on my parents. In fact, Dad keeps a copy of the letter in his office desk today. It is amazing how something as simple as a letter or essay has the power to inspire someone tremendously by tapping into their emotions, providing them with encouragement, and offering them much-needed encouragement at their most desperate times.

In September 2006, Sacia Flowers, a sixteen-year-old girl from Marysville, Washington, decided to write a letter to J. K. Rowling, the author of the Harry Potter books. Sacia (pronounced Say-sha) had a very difficult childhood. Her parents were both addicted to drugs. In fact, her mother was convicted of using cocaine eight months before she was born. Sacia was her mother's fifth child; the first three had been placed in foster care. Her mother had twins when Sacia was four. Sacia and her older sister raised their younger siblings because her mother wasn't around much. The family moved often in an attempt to hide from drug dealers, law enforcement, and social services.

"People say, 'Wasn't that hard for you to deal with?' but I didn't know any different," Sacia told the *Everett Herald*. "I didn't have a point of reference to know that's not how normal people live. I thought most families did drugs. I thought most kids were left alone a lot."[5]

Sacia's life turned even more tragic. Her father had been found dead in the family's rental home when she was nine months old. The coroner ruled his death a suicide; family members believed a drug dealer murdered him. Then, when Sacia was thirteen, her mother was murdered. A man walking a dog on a trail in a state park found her body.[6]

At school, Sacia was bullied for being smart and wearing short hair. She found comfort in reading books and loved the Harry Potter series. So much so that she decided to write a letter to Rowling to thank her for creating the skinny, black-haired, bespectacled boy who became a wizard and inspired millions of children around the world. Sacia was one of them. Like Harry Potter, she was an orphan after her parents were murdered. She had green eyes and wore glasses like him. In her letter to Rowling, Sacia called Potter her "best friend":

> Being picked on most of my life, I never had many friends due to my own insecurities and fear of loss, but through the most difficult times in my life, Harry was my best friend when I needed him most and he lent me his world in which to escape

> my own grief and hurt, and for this I thank you from the deepest part of my heart. To me, it's like Harry and I grew up together. I have grown a lot emotionally over the years and am now sixteen (as is Harry). Thank you so very much for lending me your hero and his world. He is my hero, and you are my heroine.[7]

Sacia closed the letter by telling Rowling that she did not expect a reply. She knew the author probably received thousands of fan letters. She only hoped that Rowling would read her letter. Rowling did more than that. She wrote Sacia back. Rowling had dealt with her own struggles. While she was writing the manuscript for the first Harry Potter book, her mother died of multiple sclerosis in December 1990. She had never shared the idea of her book with her mother. She was struggling emotionally and financially.

After Rowling finally finished what would become *Harry Potter and the Sorcerer's Stone*, twelve publishers turned her down before one finally agreed to buy it. It became the most famous children's book in history. In Rowling's letter to Sacia, she wrote that she had been the victim of bullying as a child too:

> I know what it is like to be picked on, as it happened to me, too, throughout my adolescence. I can only wish that you have the same

> experience that I did, and become happier and more secure the older you get. Being a teenager can be completely horrible, and many of the most successful people I know felt the same way. I think the problem is that adolescence, though often misrepresented as a time of rebellion and unconventionality, actually requires everybody to conform if they aspire to popularity—or at least to "rebel" while wearing the "right" clothes!
>
> You're now standing on the threshold of a very different phase in your life, one where you are much more likely to find kindred spirits, and much less likely to be subject to the pressures of your earlier teenage years.[8]

Receiving the letter from Rowling was a turning point in Sacia's life. Despite everything that happened, she was determined to make something better for herself and her brothers and sisters. She never used drugs or drank alcohol. She coped with her challenges by studying hard in school. She graduated second in her class in high school and received a scholarship in the honors program at Western Washington University.

"I want to do something to make a difference and leave the world a little brighter," Sacia told the *Everett Herald*. "I don't want to walk through life without someone knowing I was here."[9]

Isn't that what we all want? To make a positive impact on others and inspire people who might need it most. Words are powerful, whether they're spoken or written. I know my parents' lives changed when I was born, and Emily Kingsley's essay provided them with a roadmap for making sure I had everything I needed to overcome my medical challenges and learning differences that I'll tell you about later. J. K. Rowling's heartfelt response to a teenage girl across the pond made an indelible impact

Words are powerful, whether they're spoken or written.

on Sacia's life and inspired her to do what so many others probably believed she couldn't because of her tough circumstances.

Inspire someone to reach his or her full potential. Encourage them to be better. The author and motivational speaker Dr. Ivan Misner might have said it best when he encouraged people to change the world by changing their words: "I want someone to look at you and say, because of you, I didn't give up. Because of you,

I've learned so much more. Because of you, I'm a better leader. Because of you, I'm a success today."[10]

CHAPTER THREE

PRAY FOR SOMEONE

FAITH IS A BIG PART OF MY FAMILY'S STORY. My parents were raised in Christian homes, they prayed and read the Bible regularly, and attended church as a family almost every Sunday when I was a kid. We still do today! My relationship with God is the most important thing in my life.

I know one thing: I'm living, breathing proof of the power of prayer. VATER syndrome is a bit of a medical mystery. A child born with at least *three* of the five defects—vertebrae, anus, trachea, esophagus, and renal system—is diagnosed with VATER syndrome. In my case, I had all of them. Yep, I hit the lottery you didn't really want to win.

I was diagnosed with VATER on the first day of my life and spent my first five days on a ventilator. Since I was so sick, I was monitored in the neonatal intensive care unit twenty-four hours a day. My parents were blindsided, but because of their faith they say they didn't immediately question why their son had to be the sickly one. They knew God was in charge, that nothing happens without His direction, and that He had a plan for our lives. Wherever that plan took my parents and me, we had to trust that it was perfect and good.

My relationship with God is the most important thing in my life.

My parents quickly learned that in our weakest moments, it can feel like nobody truly understands what we're going through. My parents sometimes felt alone, even though they had each other, during what should have been the happiest times of their lives. They couldn't show off their new baby boy to family and friends because I was in the NICU. Because I was born three weeks early, Dad attended a previously scheduled baby shower for Mom. He could only show her friends a Polaroid photograph of me. There was a feeding tube in my nose, heart monitors on my chest, and a cute panda sticker covering my belly button.

Some of my parents' friends didn't call or visit because they didn't know how to act or what to say to someone who had just welcomed a sick child. My parents didn't have all the answers, either. They were scared and confused, but they placed my life in God's hands.

During those challenging times, my parents found strength in their faith and the power of prayer. So many good-hearted people were praying for me in those first few days. Mom kept all the cards and letters they received after I was born. The handwritten messages offered them much-needed encouragement, comfort, and love.

God wants us to communicate with Him through prayer. He is always there listening when we pray. Prayer can bless you, your family, and the people you pray for. Praying brings peace into your life, provides you with a better understanding of God's plan for you, and brings you closer to Him. Through prayer, we can find answers to difficult questions and avoid temptations and making the wrong decisions. Each time I pray to God, I find direction and peace.

There is plenty of proof about the power of prayer. One of my favorite movies is *Breakthrough*, which is based on the incredible true story of John Smith, a fourteen-year-old boy from St. Louis, Missouri, who fell through a frozen lake on January 19, 2015.

On that cold winter day, John and two of his friends were walking across Lake Sainte Louise when they fell through the ice. One of John's friends managed to swim to shore, while the other clung to ice. John fought as hard as he could to survive in the freezing water. Eventually, hypothermia overtook John and he went under. First responders said he was submerged for fifteen minutes before help arrived.

"I remember the screams," John told an audience at

Through prayer, we can find answers to difficult questions.

the Unity Foundation luncheon in Alexandria, Minnesota, in February 2020. "I remember the ice piercing my skin and how cold it was. I remember how it went from cold to hot real quick because of hypothermia. It was burning until I just went numb."[11]

Paramedics on the scene administered CPR but couldn't bring John back. He was rushed to a hospital, where doctors continued life-saving measures for twenty-seven minutes with no luck. Doctors said John didn't have a pulse for forty-five minutes. They were ready to pronounce him dead. Then John's mother, Joyce Smith, walked into the trauma room and began praying for her son loudly. They told Joyce there was nothing else they could do. She grabbed John's feet and made one last plea to God to bring him back. His heart started beating again.

"He was dead. But God had everything under control. He had everything in order," Joyce said.[12] Joyce truly believes that the power of God went through her and into her son.

Machines in the trauma room started beeping loudly. Suddenly, dozens of doctors were in the room, frantically working to save John. His body temperature was eighty-eight degrees, and doctors knew he wasn't out of the woods yet.

John woke up three days later. His tracheotomy was removed after a week. The most amazing part was that John's brain function was normal. He left the hospital after sixteen days. John had months of outpatient therapy, but he went on to live a normal life after his brush with death. He went to college to become a pastor. He married his high school sweetheart. He and his mother wrote a book about the harrowing incident. The book became a movie.

"Prayer is powerful," Joyce said. "We prayed for John. We wanted John to walk out of the hospital and he did."[13]

Again, millions of people around the world witnessed the power of prayer during a Monday Night Football game on January 2, 2023. Buffalo Bills safety Damar Hamlin collapsed on the field after tackling Cincinnati Bengals wide receiver Tee Higgins on what looked to be a routine play.

After the tackle, players immediately called for trainers, as Hamlin lay motionless on the field. Doctors would later determine that Hamlin had suffered cardiac arrest. Higgins's right shoulder hit Hamlin in the chest before they fell to the ground. Hamlin quickly got to his feet, then fell backward. Emergency personnel administered CPR for several minutes and eventually restored Hamlin's heartbeat on the field. Players on both teams stood around him in disbelief. Several players were crying, as were fans in the stadium, some of them reciting the Lord's Prayer.

Hamlin was given oxygen, and paramedics loaded him onto an ambulance to take him to a nearby hospital. The game was delayed and then eventually canceled. Players went on social media and asked fans to pray for Hamlin. The next day, Dan Orlovsky, a former NFL quarterback, bowed his head and prayed for Hamlin on live TV. "God, we come to You in these moments we don't understand. I believe in prayer, we believe in prayer, and we lift up Damar Hamlin's name in Your name."[14]

The day after the game, the Bills announced that Hamlin was still in critical condition and was sedated.

Fans held vigils in Cincinnati and Orchard Park, New York, where the Bills held practices. Fans raised more than $9 million in donations for Hamlin's toy drive for kids in his hometown.

On January 4, 2023, Hamlin slowly started to wake up. He communicated with his family by writing. The first thing he asked was: "Did we win?" Two days later, Hamlin was taken off a ventilator. He joined a team meeting via videoconference and told his teammates, "Love you boys." He was discharged from a hospital in Cincinnati and transferred to a facility in Buffalo, New York. On January 11, 2023, doctors announced the unbelievable news that they expected Hamlin to make a full recovery.

Miraculously, Hamlin returned to football and eased into preseason practices. On July 31, 2023, he participated in his first full-padded practice. He told reporters afterward, "This is just another milestone on the journey–might be one of the biggest ones. My faith is stronger than any fear."[15] Hamlin made the roster and participated in a game for the first time against the Miami Dolphins on October 1, 2023.

While speaking at an NFL Honors gala in Phoenix, Arizona, during Super Bowl week in February 2023, Hamlin thanked the emergency medical personnel and doctors who saved his life. He also gave a shout out to everyone around the world who had prayed for him.

"First, I would just like to thank God for being here," Hamlin said. "Every day I'm amazed that my experiences could encourage so many others across the country and even across the world—encourage them to pray, encourage to spread love, and encourage to keep fighting no matter the circumstances.

"Sudden cardiac arrest is something I never would have chosen to be a part of my story, but that's because our own visions are too small even when we think we see the bigger picture. My vision was about playing in the NFL and being the best player I could be, but God's plan was to have a purpose greater than any game in this world."[16]

We're living, breathing proof of the power of prayer and prayers of intercession. Aren't those amazing stories of hope, recovery, and faith to tell and share?

You might be surprised by some of the famous people who turn to prayer in their times of need. Country music stars Faith Hill and Tim McGraw say prayer is what has kept their marriage strong after more than a quarter-century. When they're performing together, they say a short prayer together before taking the stage. Chance the Rapper, who calls himself a Christian rapper, recalled his grandmother praying over him because she didn't like the path he was heading down.

"And she looked me in the eyes and she said, 'I don't like what's going on," Chance told *GQ* in 2016. "She said, 'I can see it in your eyes. I don't like this.'

And she says, 'We're gonna pray.' And she prayed for me all the time. Like, very positive things. But this time, she said, 'Lord, I pray that all things that are not like You, You take away from Chance. Make sure that he fails at everything that is not like You. Take it away. Turn it into dust.'"[17]

Initially, Chance—whose full name is Chancelor Johnathan Bennett—thought the prayer sounded more like a curse than a blessing. Nonetheless, he used it as an

Our own visions are too small even when we think we see the bigger picture.

opportunity to turn his life around. Since releasing his debut mixtape when he was nineteen in 2012, Chance has become a popular rapper, songwriter, record producer, and TV host. Chance is heavily involved in charitable work in his native Chicago through his foundation, SocialWorks. He has made big donations to the city's public schools, supported the arts, distributed sleeping bags to the homeless, and performed free concerts in Ghana. His mission goes back to that prayer from his grandmother.

"It's a heavy responsibility to be endowed with being a good person," Chance says. "But it comes from the inside, so there's nothing you can do about it other than stay on your path."[18]

Who can you pray for? When we feel inadequate and helpless to assist others in overcoming their obstacles like illness, drugs and alcohol, peer pressure, relationships, and decisions about college and life after high school, we can't forget that we have the power of prayer. By doing so, it helps us become more empathetic toward their struggles and puts us in their shoes. Most importantly, when we pray for others, we are doing what God wants us to do by demonstrating His love, mercy, and compassion. Pray for others with love and do it from the heart. If nothing else, it's the kind thing to do.

CHAPTER FOUR

INSPIRE OTHERS

By the time I was just three years old, I had spent a whopping 250 days in the hospital. Think about that: one-quarter of my life in a hospital bed, as doctors tried to figure out how to fix my plumbing. My parents' prayers were answered when they were introduced to Dr. Alberto Peña, who was a superstar in colon and rectal surgery.

Even before Dr. Peña became an internationally known pediatric surgeon, he knew the grief caused by childhood illnesses all too well. Dr. Peña was born in Mexico City and was the fourth of five children. Tragically, three other siblings born before him didn't make it past toddlerhood.

Dr. Peña's parents split up when he was five years old, and he went to live with his mother. His family moved often, forcing him to constantly change schools. At one point, Dr. Peña almost dropped out of school altogether, but eventually he not only finished high school, but he also found his calling when his older sisters met two students attending the Military Medical School in Mexico, who influenced him to become a doctor. Dr. Peña joined the army and enrolled in medical school. His mentor, Dr. Jesús Lozoya, was a big deal—a Mexican military physician, pediatrician, and politician. Dr. Lozoya had experienced the grief of losing a child. In his memory, he created a medal in his honor. Dr. Peña won the award in 1961 as the top student in his class.

Two years later, Dr. Peña started his surgical training at Central Military Hospital, where he spent four years. Then he made his way to University Hospital in Ann Arbor, Michigan, to study. Around this time, Dr. Peña and his then-wife, Rosalinda, gave birth to a son, Gustavo. He was born with a condition that scars and blocks the bile ducts inside and outside the liver. The condition, if left untreated, leads to liver failure and cirrhosis. Dr. Peña's son didn't look sick when he was born, but as his liver started failing, he became more and more jaundiced. Dr. Peña and his wife took Gustavo to see Dr. Robert Gross at Boston Children's Hospital, an expert at treating his condition.

Unfortunately, when Dr. Gross opened Gustavo's tiny stomach, he determined there was nothing that he could do. He sewed him back up. He had to deliver the devastating news to Dr. Peña and his wife that Gustavo might survive for another nine months. Liver transplants for children weren't an option back then. Gustavo lived for almost another five years, but he was constantly in pain without treatment.

"Those five years were extremely challenging for him and Rosalinda, who spent most of her time with Gustavo while I was working," Dr. Peña wrote in his autobiography, *Monologues of a Pediatric Surgeon*. "Gustavo was a sweet boy with a special, sensitive personality. He was small and fragile, yet he was always protective of his two, big, strong, younger brothers."[19]

During that time, according to Dr. Peña, his young son suffered from pneumonia, bleeding, irritability, and fractures because of his fragile bones. Sadly, Gustavo died in December 1969.

That agonizing personal experience inspired Dr. Peña to become a pediatric surgeon to help other parents avoid suffering the same heartache and grief. It lit a fire under him to improve the surgical techniques used to treat children with congenital colorectal conditions, to help kids like me who needed a fighting chance. Even after his personal tragedy, Dr. Peña wanted to serve others to make their lives better.

In 1972, Dr. Peña returned to Mexico City to work as the surgeon-in-chief at the new National Institute of Pediatrics. Eight years later, he revolutionized a new way to help kids like me. The new technique is commonly referred to as the Peña procedure, and doctors around the world are still using it to improve patients' lives. After moving to the United States, Dr. Peña has saved thousands of lives. He has taught the technique to hundreds of surgeons.

Dr. Peña and his wife, Andrea Bischoff, another colorectal surgeon, are still helping children at the International Center for Colorectal and Urogenital Care at Children's Hospital Colorado. Can you think of a better way to serve than saving the life of a child? I know I will forever be grateful to him for making my life so much better.

Believe it or not, Dr. Peña's impact extends beyond that. He is also inspiring his former patients and their families to become the next doctors and researchers to find cures for pediatric diseases. One of his former patients, Darius Ziabakhsh, of Vernon, New Jersey, was born with VACTER condition, which is VATER with the C of cardiac system or heart added. Darius's spine wasn't fully developed, which caused some of his other internal organs not to form properly. Almost immediately, doctors told Darius's parents, Traci Smith and Mehdi Ziabakhsh, to go see Dr. Peña, who was working at Cincinnati Children's Hospital at the time.

Darius had spinal surgery when he was four months old. When Darius was two years old, Dr. Peña was scheduled to perform a pull-through surgery. Two days before the procedure, a radiologist accidentally ruptured Darius's colon. Dr. Peña had to perform emergency surgery to remove much of his colon and repair what was left. Darius was in a coma for two weeks, and doctors weren't sure he would survive.

Darius did survive but it wasn't the end of his medical challenges. By the time he was nine years old, he had endured thirty medical procedures, including ten major surgeries.

Darius and his family spent a lot of time at the Ronald McDonald House in Cincinnati while Dr. Peña was caring for him. In 2016, Ronald McDonald House

Can you think of a better way to serve than saving the life of a child?

Charities surprised Darius by sending him to the Summer Olympics in Rio de Janeiro. He learned of the trip while standing on the field at a New York Red Bulls soccer game. Not only was Darius going to attend the Rio Olympics, but also he and other children from around the world were going to walk in the opening ceremonies. It was an experience of a lifetime.

Darius's older brother CJ was so inspired by Ronald McDonald Charities' kindness that he decided to host a

Thanksgiving dinner at the Ronald McDonald House in New Brunswick, New Jersey. CJ and his father still host a holiday dinner for three hundred people, including first responders, at a Ronald McDonald House in New York. In addition to Dr. Peña, Darius says his older brother is his biggest inspiration.

CJ, or Colin, is studying microbiology and molecular biology at Rutgers University in Piscataway, New Jersey. He plans to apply to medical school to become a doctor.

So, in my mind, I'm always reflecting on what's good, the good I can get out of a situation, or recognizing the good at that moment.

CJ is on two research teams trying to find a cure for Down syndrome.

"Darius and Dr. Peña were both his inspiration, so they're inspiring each other," Traci said.

Darius plans to follow in his brother's footsteps and attend medical school too. He wants to become a pediatrician or pediatric surgeon to help kids like us.

For now, he's counseling younger children who have been diagnosed with VACTER and other medical conditions.

"If I can get to people and tell them how I've overcome my medical hardships and help them make their lives better, that makes me feel amazing," Darius said.

Traci is also doing much to help parents of children with colorectal disorders. When Darius was born, the Internet wasn't in every home, so she couldn't jump on Google to learn more about his condition. She couldn't reach out to other parents who had endured similar situations because there wasn't a directory available. So, Traci founded the Colorectal Support Network, which has more than 1,300 members in seventy-five countries around the world.

The most important thing Darius and his family can pass along to others is his positive outlook.

"I've always believed that whenever I'm having a surgery or I notice something is wrong, there's no reason to focus on the negatives," Darius said. "That's just going to make it worse. So, in my mind, I'm always reflecting on what's good, the good I can get out of a situation, or recognizing the good at that moment."[20]

How can you inspire others like Darius and Dr. Peña? You don't have to be a doctor to do it. You can inspire by spreading positivity and caring for others. Be empathetic. Be gracious. Be enthusiastic. Hold up others and inspire them to be themselves. Build up their confidence. You'll be surprised how much of an impact you can make by just being kind.

CHAPTER FIVE

BE A FRIEND

I'VE KNOWN MY BEST FRIEND IN THE WORLD, THOMAS Stevenson, since we were toddlers. He was born about a month before me. My dad, Jim, played sports in high school with his father, Tom. Since we were so close in age, my mom became good friends with his mother, Colleen. Our families had dinner together, our parents attended the same Bible studies, and we took vacations together.

When we were kids, our mothers took turns babysitting, and more times than not we ended up at my house for play dates because at least once or twice each day, I'd have to head for the bathroom for an hour-long enema to let my body do its thing.

My colostomy bag had been reversed when I was just over a year old, and by this time I had to give myself enemas lying on the ground and catheterize myself. It took forever, and sometimes didn't work, which meant I had to do it all over again. When I was ten years old, I had the Malone procedure, which rerouted everything through my belly button. It was a faster process and not nearly as uncomfortable. In fact, I still must do it every day.

So, here's the deal: When it's time to use the restroom, I mix a concoction of glycerin, Dr. Bronner's Pure-Castile Liquid Soap, and water in an IV bag. The fluids flush me out—top to bottom—through my small intestine, colon, rectum, anus, and eventually into the toilet. It typically takes about thirty to forty minutes, but if my stools are hard and the fluids won't work it can be a daylong affair. On those days, I might start the enema at seven o'clock in the morning and not finish until four o'clock in the afternoon. It's not much fun and it wears me down.

But you know what? It's still better than having to use a colostomy bag, that's for sure. Ask my former babysitter, Sarah Kennedy Gilpin, who started caring for me when I was still using one. At the time, Sarah was only fifteen years old, and she became a member of our family and one of my closest friends. Sarah wanted to be a nurse and had a heart of gold. Sometimes, if I were playing too hard, the colostomy bag would fall off. On rare occasions, the bag would explode—sometimes all over poor Sarah! There were a few nights my parents came home to find Sarah wearing Mom's clothes.

Sarah's married now and her daughter, Lauren, is diabetic. Sarah says her time with me helped prepare her for raising a child with diabetes. She says I taught her to be patient and flexible. She appreciated how I overcame the difficult times in life, with little to no complaining, no matter the obstacle. Sarah knows that she and Lauren will get through rough patches, just like I did.

One day, when I was in elementary school, I was playing with my next-door neighbor, Stephen, when Dad yelled that it was time for my enema. I told Stephen goodbye and ran inside. Our phone rang a few minutes later. It was Stephen's mother. "Stephen just asked me when he gets to do his enema," his mother said.

Stephen's mother didn't know the full extent of my medical problems. They both agreed that Stephen probably wouldn't want one! From that day forward, Dad started calling my enema a "treatment," so it wouldn't confuse my friends.

While the smell and sounds of an enema would gross out most kids and send them running for the hills, my friend Thomas was patient and simply shrugged it off. He even sat on the bathroom floor waiting for me to finish. Eventually, Mom put a desk in the bathroom for us. I sat on my throne waiting to drop off the kids with a towel over my lap, while Thomas sat at the desk across from me. We played LEGOs, Matchbox cars, Playmobil, or Rescue Heroes to pass the time. Thomas sat right there with me, day after day, and didn't think twice about it.

When it was time for me to finish, Thomas left the room. Then, we picked up where we left off. That's the thing I'll always love about Thomas—he never treated me differently because of my medical differences, never teased me about them, and just never thought much about it.

During the spring and summer, when the weather was nice in Michigan, Thomas and I built forts and tents on top of the shed behind my house, complete with a pulley system to get everything we needed up there. On any given day, we were firefighters or police officers, always fighting the good fight against the bad guys. During the cold winters, we built snow forts or pitched our tents inside.

When my parents purchased the house they're still living in now, Dad gave me one room upstairs to make my own. It was basically a big closet. He said I could decorate it any way I wanted (as long as I kept the door closed). Thomas and I painted the walls, and that became our clubhouse. We even had imaginary girlfriends—I can't remember what they looked like!

In the fourth and fifth grades, Thomas and I played peewee football together for the Grosse Pointe Red Barons. Despite my small size, our coach made me the starting center. Dad reminded Coach Climm that I had short-term memory loss and might blank out on the snap count! Thomas was the nose guard, so we went head-to-head in practice every day. He wore the number

54 jersey; I wore number 55. Thomas and I also played lacrosse together for the Jays, and even though I was one of the smaller guys on the field, I wasn't afraid to get dirty and scoop up ground balls, which can be dangerous. As you might imagine, even though I was smaller than other kids my age, I didn't back down from anyone. I wasn't frail or anything like that, and my speed and desire compensated for what I might have lacked in size and strength.

Each summer, Thomas and I left for a week to attend the SpringHill Camp in Evart, Michigan. It's an interdenominational Christian camp that has been around for more than four decades. We had an absolute blast there! We had Skittle Skattle Battles through the hills and woods surrounding the camp; it was our own version of Capture the Flag with snack-size bags of Skittles, which we hurled about one hundred miles per hour at each other. We went horseback riding and tubing on the lake. There was a rock wall to climb and even a zipline. We played just about every single sport; boredom was definitely not on the calendar. It was such a wonderful place for kids to spend the summer.

Thomas and I slept in the same cabin at SpringHill Camp, and that's where we talked to the older counselors about faith and read Scripture. Thomas was right next to me the night I professed my faith in Jesus Christ while we were sitting around a crackling campfire. I'd been baptized as a baby and my family went to a church regularly, but as I grew older, I began to understand more about my faith, especially given the physical ailments I'd had to endure. I knew I loved Jesus and He had a plan for me, whatever it was.

Now, let me introduce you to another one of my closest friends, who's really more like a brother, Gregory Nelson. Our families are super tight. In fact, he calls my mother his "mom," and I call his mother my "mom." Our families are *that* close. During the summers when we were growing up, Gregory and I practically lived at the Old Club, which is located on Harsens Island in the Lake St. Clair Flats. We mostly go to the Old Club via our boat, and it's so close to Canada that you can hit Windsor, Ontario, by skipping a stone.

The Old Club, as you might guess, is ancient. It was founded in 1872 by a group of industrialists from Detroit who pitched in $25 for shares of the Lake St. Clair Fishing and Shooting Club of Detroit. It had a small dock and twenty-six boathouses. Eventually, it became a social gathering spot and retreat for many families who built summer homes there. In 1902, it was re-christened as the Old Club, and it's still there more than one hundred years later. Even now, we spend quite a bit of time at the Old Club, boating, fishing, shooting skeet, and swimming in the pool.

One of the best things about living in Grosse Pointe Farms, Michigan, is fishing and boating on Lake St. Clair, which is sometimes referred to as the

"Sixth Great Lake." It's not nearly as big as the other five, covering only 430 square miles, and it isn't nearly as deep. But it still provides great freshwater fishing and boating. It was an endless playground for me while I was growing up.

Gregory and I grew up on the water together. As soon as we could swim, we were spending summer days on the lake fishing for bass, walleye, pike, and muskellunge. Some days, we'd catch a boatload of fish. Other days, we wouldn't catch anything but still had tall fish tales to share. Nowadays, if we're not fishing together, Gregory and I have one rule between us: If there's no photo, there's no proof. We sailed and boated when we were kids, and we still ride Jet Skis together. We're like Goose and Maverick from *Top Gun* on the water.

I knew I loved Jesus and He had a plan for me, whatever it was.

Of course, life changes and we grow up fast. When I went away to college, Gregory attended Michigan State University and Thomas left for Rollins College in

Florida. Fortunately, each of us moved back home after graduation and still see each other quite a bit.

True friends are authentic and honest. They're your friends when you're around them and when you're not. We all want to experience the feeling of community, whether it's on a team, in a club or social group, with friends at work, or at youth group at church. If you want people to be around you, then you need to be a happy and kind person. Reflect on the characteristics of who you want to be, and choose friends who are like that.

Your best friends are the ones who are difficult to find, impossible to leave, and whom you will never forget.

Your best friends are the ones who are difficult to find, impossible to leave, and whom you will never forget. I guess that old Irish proverb about friends is true: A good friend is like a four-leaf clover: hard to find and lucky to have. I know I'm the luckiest man in the world.

Although you've most likely created good social relationships over the years, brushing up on your friendship skills can be beneficial. Having close friends gives us someone to turn to when we feel lonely, need a listening ear, or want someone to celebrate with. If you've ever had a great friend, notice all the things they did with you, for you, and on your behalf.

Studies show that America's teenagers are spending less and less time with each other. They've traded actual face-to-face time for FaceTime, TikTok, YouTube, Snapchat, and other social media. The COVID-19 pandemic didn't help.

"Teens are spending a lot more time communicating with each other electronically and a lot less time hanging out with each other face to face," said Jean Twenge, a professor of psychology at San Diego State University and author of *Generations*, a book about generational differences. "Going to the mall has gone down. Driving in the car for fun has gone down. Going to the movies has gone down. We're talking about kids who are spending five, six, seven hours a day on social media."[21]

In May 2023, United States Surgeon General Vivek Murthy declared loneliness to be a national epidemic. His eighty-two-page report noted that loneliness can lead to a 29-percent increase in the risk of heart disease, 32-percent increased risk of stroke, and a 50-percent increased risk of developing dementia for older adults.[22]

"Given the significant health consequences of loneliness and isolation, we must prioritize building social connection the same way we have prioritized other critical public health issues such as tobacco use, obesity, and substance use disorders," Murthy said in a statement. "Together, we can build a country that's healthier, more resilient, less lonely, and more connected."[23]

There's simply no substitute for face-to-face interaction. It doesn't take much effort to get together with your friends. Ask them to go hiking or go for a bike ride. Ask them to join you when you're running around town. Take a walk in a park or nature area. Work on a project together, whether it's something for school or a hobby both of you enjoy. A study by the *Journal of the American Geriatrics Society* showed that people who get together regularly with family and friends are about half as likely to report symptoms of depression as those who have little face-to-face contact. Hanging out with your friends is a vitamin for loneliness and depression.

Whether you're learning to be that kind of a friend yourself or you just want to polish up your "good friend" skills, these ideas might help you establish and maintain positive, fulfilling friendships. Be a good listener. Everyone has times when we just want to vent. When you make the decision to listen rather than offer feedback or suggestions, you're practicing one of the most important behaviors of a good friend. Keep your ears and mind open. Remember to support your friends. Be someone your friend can count on. Be dependable and predictable in your friendship. Doing so will ensure that you'll never have a shortage of people who care for you.

Your time is even more valuable than your words. We all lead busy lives but make a commitment to spend time with your friends: cheer for your school's teams, go out for dinner, go thrift shopping, wash your cars, or just hang out. A good friend wants to be together and makes time in a busy schedule to do it. Be creative in the planning of activities and you'll make great memories.

Being a great friend will bring you moments of joy,

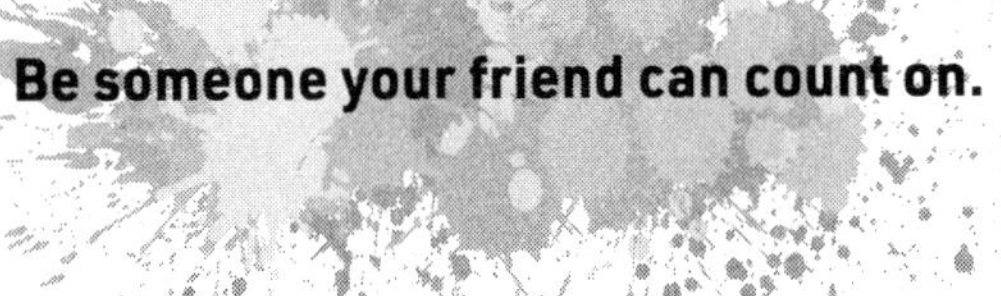

years of comfort, and decades of cherished memories. Implement these strategies in your relationships today. You will feel like you're the best friend ever and those you care about will think so too!

CHAPTER SIX

CREATE MEMORIES

IMAGINE WAKING UP EVERY MORNING AND NOT remembering what you did the day before. Or walking into a Chipotle and not recalling that you like black beans but can't stand pintos. Or you constantly forget how to make your way around a *Fortnite* map even though you've played the game hundreds of times. Or, for the life of you, you can't remember the lyrics to your favorite Taylor Swift song, like "Blank Space."

Sometimes, my mind felt like a blank space when I was a kid. As the opening lyrics of that song go, some mornings I woke up, looked in the mirror, and said, "Nice to meet you, where you been?" You see, along with the laundry list of serious medical issues I faced as a child, I also suffered from short-term memory loss, which made learning to read and write quite difficult when I was young. It's not like I had amnesia or blackouts, but I struggled to remember lessons I'd learned in school only hours before.

My mother first picked up on the problem when I was about five years old. I was enrolled at the Montessori Early School at Grosse Pointe Academy in Grosse Pointe Farms, Michigan. One afternoon, while Mom and I waited in the long carpool lane after school, she began pointing out my classmates and asking me their names.

Sometimes, my mind felt like a blank space when I was a kid.

No matter how hard I tried, I couldn't remember them. I couldn't even recall my teacher's name. They were like strangers, even though I interacted with them every day in class and on the playground.

At home, I couldn't remember the words to simple songs we had been singing in class. I couldn't recall the alphabet, even though Mom and I had been reciting it together for months. Mom and I read "Jack and Jill" repeatedly at bedtime. When she'd ask me about the poem we'd just read, I'd only remember that Jack and Jill went up the hill—not that Jack fell down and Jill came tumbling after. It was the same scenario with "Humpty Dumpty." I remembered that he sat on a wall, but that was the end of the story for me.

When Mom and Dad approached my preschool teacher about their concerns, she brushed it off as absent-mindedness and nothing to be too concerned about. But my ability to remember names and facts didn't improve over the next few months, and my parents weren't going to ignore the problem. Mom and Dad scheduled a conference with the head of the school. After several meetings, he suggested that maybe the Montessori early school wasn't the right place for me.

Seriously? Nope, my parents weren't having that. They have always been my biggest advocates, and they were going to do everything in their power to put me in the best academic environment possible.

After preschool, I jumped to another school, University Liggett School in Grosse Pointe Woods. It was only in the first few weeks of classes there that my first-grade teacher, Peggy Dettlinger, recognized the same red flags. I wasn't acting out, and I followed her instructions. I paid attention in class as much as any six-year-old kid could. Yet, I was struggling to complete my work. Over the next few months, my learning differences had Mrs. Dettlinger and other teachers at University Liggett School scratching their heads.

My parents recognized other problems at home. I couldn't remember letters or numbers well. I couldn't memorize our home phone number, address, or even 911. As difficult as reading was for me, I also struggled with math because the symbols for adding, subtracting, dividing, and multiplying just didn't stick in my noggin. I forgot the signs that identified the men's and women's restrooms at restaurants and school—talk about embarrassing!

I loved banging on my keyboard as a kid, but when my parents signed me up for piano lessons, it was a lost cause because I couldn't remember the notes, let alone read sheet music. Dance classes? Same thing: I couldn't remember the steps. I loved sports and played football, lacrosse, and just about everything else, but my parents couldn't figure out why I disliked tae kwon do so much. It took them more than a year to discover the problem. Turns out, I couldn't remember to bow to my instructors and opponents, how to sit inside the dojang, or any of the other rituals that are associated with the martial art.

If you were like me as a kid, you probably loved the Disney movies *Finding Nemo* and *Finding Dory.* My favorite character was the blue tang fish Dory. Her brain kind of worked like mine; it was wired a little differently. Dory was able to recall memories of her parents and where they lived when she was a child. But ask her Nemo's name or where they're headed, and it's crickets. Yep, sometimes I can relate to exactly how Dory felt.

Now, I'm not much of a "chick flick" fan, but one movie that really resonated with me as a teenager was *50 First Dates.* It is about a veterinarian named Henry who falls in love after meeting a teacher named Lucy in a restaurant. Adam Sandler, one of my favorite actors, plays the role of Henry. Drew Barrymore is Lucy in the movie.

Here's how the plot goes: Henry talks Lucy into having breakfast with him, they connect instantly, and she agrees to meet him again the next morning. But when Henry shows up the next day, Lucy freaks out and says she's never met him. Restaurant employees tell Henry that Lucy was seriously injured in a car wreck and suffers from amnesia. She remembers all the details of her life up until the night before the accident. She can make new memories each day, but then loses them when she goes to sleep. Henry is still determined to win her over, even if he must start from scratch every morning. Don't worry; I won't spoil the ending if you haven't seen the movie before.

It wasn't as if I had amnesia like Lucy. I knew my parents, my dog Duke, my friends, and grandparents. I hadn't forgotten who they were or the events that had shaped my life to that point. I could remember what I'd done at school that day and what I'd eaten for dinner the night before. But when it came to anything I read, I forgot the material only a short time later. It was like my brain didn't absorb what my eyes were reading.

Finally, in the spring of 2003, University Liggett School referred my parents to Dr. Marquita Bedway, a well-respected educational psychologist. She put me through a battery of tests, observed me in the classroom, and interviewed my parents and teachers. In her final report, Dr. Bedway determined that my general cognitive ability was in the high average range of intellectual functioning, and my nonverbal reasoning abilities were

It was like my brain didn't absorb what my eyes were reading.

superior. However, something was misfiring in my brain, which wasn't allowing me to learn how to read and write, or how to memorize letters, numbers, and symbols.

Basically, what Dr. Bedway determined was that my functional IQ was 115, which doctors consider superior intelligence and high—but not higher than most other people. When it came to reading, spelling, and math, however, my scores were borderline or low average. I simply couldn't remember words, numbers, or symbols because of short-term memory loss.

In December 2003, the Grosse Pointe Public School System agreed to evaluate my needs for special services. The evaluation confirmed Dr. Bedway's assessment and what my parents and teachers already knew: My educational achievement was very low. My very first IEP included preferential seating, modified assignments, oral testing, and longer time for tests. Those were the only things the district recommended at the time.

Unless you've been in the shoes of someone struggling to learn how to read, you can't grasp how painful it can be. I recognized letters while trying to read, but remembering the sounds they made was an entirely different ball game. Once I mastered the phonetics of the alphabet, I struggled to put letters together to build words or put words together to construct sentences. Even after I learned to read, which was a long and hard process (more on that in the next chapter), I still struggled to remember what I'd just read because of my short-term memory loss. I'd read a few sentences from a book and then, poof, gone.

It's the same way with video games. When I was younger, I spent hours playing *Madden NFL*, *Call of Duty*, *Forza Motorsport*, and other video games with my friends. My buddies probably loved playing *Madden NFL* against me because I couldn't remember what play I had selected only a few seconds earlier, which typically led to a turnover or busted assignment. Even reading words like start, exit, and pause on the TV was a puzzle.

Board games weren't something we did as a family. Kids games like *Concentration*, *Memory Game*, and other card games were too frustrating for me. Sometimes, when I'm at a friend's house for the holidays, I'll sit back and watch them play games because it's too difficult for me to remember the instructions. Thankfully, I have some awesome friends who asked me to team up with them to keep me involved and not feel left out.

One silver lining about having short-term memory is that I've never been much of a gambler because of my circumstances. In a card game like Blackjack, I can't remember that an ace is worth one or eleven or that face cards are worth ten. Las Vegas would throw an epic party if I bellied up to a table from time to time!

When Mom sends me to the grocery store to pick up a few things, she makes sure to write me a list. Without one, I'll usually come home without at least one thing she wanted. That happens to all of us from time to time, but it happens to me often if I don't take a list.

Here's what my family and I have learned over the years: My memory is much better if I've experienced and visualized something. Even though I might not remember the names of streets or places, I remember how to get there. When we were driving to northern Michigan to go boating in the summer or skiing in the winter, I'd often remind my parents about an upcoming turn or exit. If a friend called and asked me to meet them for lunch, I might not have remembered the name of a particular restaurant, but I knew it was a brunch place across the street from a park or a cozy coffee shop near the library. I can tell you most of the intimate details about family vacations and other events because I experienced them and lived them.

Of course, my short-term memory loss was much more of a concern when I was a kid. My parents and teachers had to come up with a game plan to tackle the problem. I wanted to learn to read and write more than anything. Even though I wasn't nearly as good a reader as the other children in my class, I was super eager to learn. At first, I was nervous about reading in front of my classmates. Fortunately, most of them encouraged me despite my struggles.

Two years after the Grosse Pointe Public School System rolled out an IEP program to help me learn, administrators called my parents to an annual meeting in 2005. The head of the University Liggett Lower School was there, along with a special education teacher and my teachers from the third and fourth grades. A learning specialist, speech pathologist, district representative, and school psychologist also attended the meeting.

Over the previous several months, my parents tried everything to help me learn to read and write, including specialized reading programs, tutors, and much prayer. Students in my classes were already reading chapter books, while I was still struggling to spell and read simple words. No matter what my parents and I tried, we were stuck in a never-ending struggle.

During the meeting, the Grosse Pointe public school psychologist laid out the results of my tests and shared what she had observed while visiting my classroom. Then, she just stopped. My parents will always remember the bombshell that came next: "Mr. and Mrs. Mestdagh, it's my conclusion that JT is illiterate and always will be. He will never learn to read. You as a family need to accept that and to learn how to cope going forward."

Tears filled my parents' eyes, as the psychologist hurriedly suggested a few special schools for students like me. Then, Dad interrupted her.

"JT will learn to read," he said. "We will find a way to help him learn to read."

And with that, the meeting was over.

When was the last time you stood up for someone? Standing up for someone, especially when they're being bullied or mistreated, is not only our moral responsibility and the right thing to do, but it also helps foster a more compassionate world. It's the kind thing to do. Standing up for others promotes justice, builds empathy, fosters inclusivity, promotes social change, and sets an example for others.

The term "upstander" has become popular among educators and psychologists in recent years. An upstander is someone who recognizes when something is wrong and takes action to make it right. Upstanders are good people who will do something, no matter how their peers might perceive them, to stop bullying or other mistreatment. It's easy to be an upstander. Respect others' differences. Be kind and compassionate to everyone. Have empathy for others. Don't spread hurtful rumors about others. Reach out to a new kid in your class and make them feel included. Introduce those being bullied to your friends. Don't encourage people who are being mean. If a classmate is

Family is God's greatest blessing to us, and family is the anchor that holds us through life's storms.

being bullied, talk to them and be a friend. Praise others who stop bullying and do the right thing.

One of the most memorable scenes in *Finding Dory* is when Dory says, "Good question. See, I can remember some things because well ... uh, they make sense. Like, um, I have a family. I know because I've—I put have come from somewhere, right? Everyone has a family. I may not remember their names and what they look like. And I may not even be able to ever find them again. But, um ... what were we talking about?"[24]

Despite struggling to remember many things, Dory never forgot that she had a family out there somewhere in the deep blue sea. If nothing else, she remembered that her parents loved her and she loved them. Family is God's greatest blessing to us, and family is the anchor that holds us through life's storms. True friends can be just as important, especially those who have your back and are willing to stand up for you.

My parents waited several years to share the details of that meeting at school with me. By that time, I already knew that they were never going to give up on me. That's something I will never forget.

CHAPTER SEVEN

TAKE OFF YOUR MASK

WHO DIDN'T GET SICK AND TIRED OF HAVING TO wear a mask in public during the recent pandemic? We all had to cover our faces to slow down the spread of COVID-19 when we couldn't maintain our distance, whether it was when we were picking up groceries, chowing down at a restaurant, chilling in class, or riding on public transportation. And, let's face it, those masks didn't just protect us from COVID-19; they also hid how truly terrible our morning breath is!

Now, let me tell you about a different kind of mask—the one that's preventing you from becoming your true, authentic self. I'm referring to the disguise you might wear to fit in with the cool kids at school you really want to join, or the one to hide your insecurities. Those masks are preventing you from being who you truly are and reaching your full potential. While superheroes like

Spider-Man, Wolverine, and Cyclops wore a mask to protect their identities, the masks we sometimes wear might strip us of our superpowers. You know what? Stan Lee, the iconic comic book writer and editor, once said Spider-Man wore a mask so enemies couldn't see his fear. See, superheroes are just like us.

Being real and original isn't easy, and you must take off your mask to do it. I know it can be downright scary and uncomfortable to think about. You've got to muster up bold courage and strength to take off a mask. Believe me, I know what it's like to take off a disguise and expose your warts to the world.

Flashback to 2006, I'm in the fifth grade, and guess what? Yep, I still can't read or write. In a journal, my mom wrote: "In school since the beginning, JT has struggled and continues to do so. His memory is an issue also. One teacher said it is like a 'stroke victim.' He has the info but he can't retrieve it. Another teacher, Mrs. [Peggy] Dettlinger, felt JT's mind is like a light switch; one day it is on and one day it is off."

Unfortunately, the switch was off most of the time. It felt like the circuit breaker to my brain had been flipped. We needed to find someone who could help us switch it back on and leave it there. Fortunately, a family friend, Kathy Genthe, introduced my parents to a man named Steve Tattum. Steve was a magician in special education after studying at Eastern Illinois University and George Washington University. He was a director of the Denver

Academy, a private day school in Colorado, where he developed the radical and amazing F.A.S.T. Reading System (now called Tattum Reading).

Turns out, Steve just so happened to be in Detroit training teachers in his program when my parents called. So, one night in September 2006, we drove to meet Steve at a hotel in Bloomfield Hills, Michigan. When we arrived at the hotel, Steve was sitting alone in a dimly

The masks we sometimes wear might strip us of our superpowers.

lit lobby. He had shaggy gray-blond hair and a mustache. Steve shook hands with Mom and Dad, and then he dropped to one knee, getting on the same level as me. "And you must be JT. Let's get started, okay?"

As Steve walked me down a hallway to a conference room he was using as his office that week, I could feel the pit in my stomach. Would this appointment be another waste of time with another educator who would reach the same conclusion as everyone else? Were my hopes and dreams going to be dashed once again? Would I ever learn to read and write? All my life, I'd felt like Neo in those Keanu Reeves movies, only I had never cracked the code to the Matrix.

On the table between us, Steve placed a flipbook. It looked exactly like all the ones that I'd used in other reading programs, which might as well have been written in German. I couldn't read them. This one had a spiral binding and bright-colored tabs. Steve used the letters to spell out simple words like *bat*, *cat*, *den*, and *pen*. My stomach was doing somersaults again. As Steve cleaned up the way I pronounced consonants and vowels, I tried to read words for about ten minutes without much luck.

Then, much to my surprise, Steve did something completely unexpected: he threw the flipbook across the room. "You'll never see that again," he promised me. I knew right then that Steve was different from anyone else I'd worked with before. I could trust him.

Steve pulled out a rectangular white board about the size of a laptop. It had small magnetic tiles of letters scattered all over it. It looked like a Scrabble board filled with jumbled words. For a few minutes, we went through what Steve called the vowel galaxy. Then, he flipped over the board.

The other side was covered with tiles made up of two to four letters like *un*, *ex*, *rupt*, *mit*, *ble*, and *tion*—organized in colors. Steve used them to spell out a word I'd never seen before. "Okay, JT. Read that one," he said.

"Un . . . rupt . . . tion," I said. "What's that mean?"

"It's a nonsense word," he told me. "But did you see what you just did? You just read a three-syllable word."

We went over "words" like *un-rupt-tion* for thirty minutes or so. Then, Steve handed me one of his books called *Ocean Fun*. He asked me to read a sentence that most first-graders could easily conquer: "It's fun in the sun." I stumbled over a couple of words, and Steve gently corrected me. He read the next two sentences. We went on like that for a page and a half. Before I knew it, I realized that I was reading!

In that very first meeting, Steve accomplished what every educator before him had failed to do: He made me believe that I could read. Now, I must tell you that because of my short-term memory problems and processing disorder, Steve said I had one of the most difficult cases of dyslexia he had ever encountered in his thirty years working with children with learning differences.

But here's the plot twist: I didn't wear camouflage to hide the problem and badly wanted to learn to read and write. I was determined to do it, no matter how hard I would have to work and how vulnerable and exposed I would feel. Sure, I was nervous and didn't want my classmates teasing me because I couldn't read and write as well as them. But I knew the result was going to be worth it.

I was so excited leaving that very first meeting with Steve. It was like a door in my brain, one that had previously been closed, had suddenly been kicked open. On the drive home that night, my parents were amazed as I sounded out the names on street signs. I spent a week working with Steve before he went back to Colorado. After only a few days, one of my teachers called Mom.

"What are you doing with JT?" she asked.

I was determined to do it, no matter how hard I would have to work and how vulnerable and exposed I would feel.

"What do you mean?" Mom replied.

The teacher had handed out a homework assignment and fully expected to have to explain to me what I was supposed to be reading. But when she came to my desk to collect my work, she was amazed that I had already answered the questions.

"Kris, he had already filled out the worksheet! I asked him how, and he said, 'I read it!' Kris, what's going on?" my teacher asked.

Steve said I was the most motivated child he had ever encountered. I wanted to read. Each night, before I went to bed, I prayed to God to allow me to read. Each year, my birthday wish was to be able to read and write. Steve's system gave me the confidence to do it. Suddenly, I had so much self-esteem. The anxiety and dread I'd had for so long was gone. I was no longer intimidated when a teacher called on me. My hands no longer sweated during tests. I knew I could do the work.

When Steve returned to Colorado, my parents arranged for me to continue working with a F.A.S.T. tutor named Susie Jacobs. I'd go to my classes at University Liggett School until 3:00 p.m., and then Mom would drive me forty-five minutes to Farmington Hills, Michigan, to work with Mrs. Susie and Deb North, another tutor who helped me with homework. After that, I'd go home for my hour-long bowel management program, followed by more homework and dinner, before finally going to bed.

Steve told my parents that I might benefit from enrolling at the Denver Academy, where I could continue to work with him. Dad couldn't move to Colorado because of work, and my parents didn't want to be separated for so long. Sending me off as a boarding student wasn't an option because of my medical issues. Since I was making good progress with the F.A.S.T. tutors, Mom and Dad decided we should continue down that road, as tiring as it was for all of us.

Then, out of the blue, everything changed. Just before Thanksgiving break during the fifth grade, I was walking down the hall when I heard a man's voice say, "JT! Got a minute?" It was the headmaster of University Liggett School. He motioned me over to a corner near the water fountain. He had his golden retriever with him; he brought the dog to school with him nearly every day. I was looking down at his dog when he delivered the devastating news.

"JT, I need to let you know that you're not reading or writing well enough for you to stay at Liggett for middle school," the headmaster told me. "You can't come here next year."

I couldn't believe my ears. He had ambushed me with the news right before the holidays. Even if it weren't a holiday, what kind of man says that to an eleven-year-old? I knew he hadn't told my parents yet, because they would have broken the news to me gently. Let me tell you, at that moment, I wished I'd had a mask to hide from him how much his words had cut.

"Yes, sir," was all I could muster before I walked slowly out the school's back door. I ran through the grassy area that separated the campus from my backyard. By the time I ran through the side door of my house, I was crying uncontrollably. The only thought in my head was that I was stupid. Mom quickly grabbed me and examined me up and down for injuries.

"JT! What happened? What's wrong?" she asked.

I was crying so hard that I couldn't answer her.

Finally, I calmed down enough to spill the beans about my conversation with the headmaster in the hall. She wanted to march over to the school and confront him right then, but she called Dad first. My parents set up a meeting with the headmaster for the next day. Guess what? He didn't bother to show up. He sent the headmaster of the lower school instead. He told my parents that the decision had already been made. I wasn't invited back to the school for the next year. I was being banished.

So, over that Christmas break, I visited Denver Academy with Mom and Dad. The teachers and students welcomed me with open arms, making me feel like I had finally found my place. We leased an apartment and rented some furniture. In January 2007, Mom and I, along with my loving dog Duke, moved to Denver. Dad came out whenever he could get away from work, which usually meant every other weekend.

One of the first things I realized about the Denver Academy was that each of the students there had some sort of learning difference, just like me. I had discovered a place where I fit in. After only a few weeks, I told Mom, "I don't feel different here. Everyone is like me." No masks needed here!

In only five months of working with Steve, his awesome assistant, Rosemarie Offenhauer (or Mrs. O, as I called her), and the other wonderful teachers and tutors at the Denver Academy, I learned to read and write. I spent each morning working with Steve and Mrs. O in the F.A.S.T. House before joining my classmates. I was reading and writing, but I hadn't yet mastered those skills. It's something I'm still working on today.

In April 2007, we flew back to Detroit, and my parents had a meeting with administrators and teachers at University Liggett School to discuss whether I could return for middle school the next year. They shared my test results and the impressive progress I'd made while working with Steve and attending the Denver Academy. But you know what? The teachers didn't say a word. The headmaster didn't show up again. My parents were told that because of my learning differences, I simply didn't fit in with the culture at University Liggett and couldn't return there.

Back at that earlier meeting with Steve and my parents in Denver, I shared something that had been weighing on my heart for a while: "My only concern is that all the other children in Michigan that struggle with reading may never get to know about F.A.S.T."

That's when my parents made it their mission to help me bring the F.A.S.T. program to schools in Michigan to help kids who are struggling with learning differences learn to read and write too. Mom and Dad made numerous phone calls and sent emails to anyone they knew in the local school systems.

Move ahead to April 23, 2007, and there I was, standing in front of the whiteboard in the field house at Grosse Pointe Academy. I scanned the room of more than one hundred adults. I recognized teachers, tutors, principals, and psychologists who had worked with me in the past. A few of them had been the ones who delivered the verdict my parents had refused to accept that I was illiterate for life.

Dad made a few opening remarks, then Steve walked to the front of the room. He took a few minutes to explain who he was and what the F.A.S.T. Reading System was about. Then, he called me up. "Let's show people how much you've learned, okay?" he said.

Steve put me through a full lesson, using the magnetic white board, as we did each morning at the F.A.S.T. House in Denver. At the ripe age of ten, I decided to take off my mask and reveal my biggest insecurity. Right there, in front of some of the very people who told my parents I'd never read or write, I mustered the strength and courage to show them how wrong they were. I'd never felt so exposed, yet so determined.

After the lesson, Steve pulled out a book, *French Quarter Phantom*, which he'd written for middle third- and beginning fourth-grade readers. I read from the book for about ten minutes. I stumbled a few times but showed the group how much I'd improved over the previous four months.

When the meeting was over, a woman from the audience came up to us. I remembered her as someone who had worked with me when I was younger.

"I'm sorry," she said. "But I find it so hard to believe that JT can read like this. I worked with him. I know where he was as a reader just months ago."

I looked at my parents. Mom was stunned the woman would suggest that I couldn't read, and that Steve and I

Be bold. Be fearless. Be courageous. Be free.

had simply memorized the sentences from the book.

Steve was calm. He simply asked the woman if she had a piece of paper with writing in her purse. She stumbled through her bag and handed him a sales receipt. He glanced at it and handed it to me. "Read it," Steve told me.

I squinted while trying to make out the small type. "Fresh Market Farms . . . cheddar cheese," I said, before moving down the receipt.

I looked up at Mom and Steve. They had wide smiles on their faces. I knew they were proud of me. The woman was smiling with tears in her eyes. After working with me for so long, she simply couldn't believe it was true. What are your insecurities? What makes you vulnerable? Why are you wearing a disguise? Remember, you don't need a physical difference to feel handicapped. If you're living a life that's not true to yourself because you're concealing your real identity, you're holding yourself back. It's a false reality. You're Batman one day, Spider-Man the next. Take off that mask. Be bold. Be fearless. Be courageous. Be free.

We all have problems and insecurities. Taking off your mask begins when you make that decision to let go of everyone and everything that no longer contributes to your growth. Take off the disguise and embrace authenticity. Authentic people stay true to themselves, which allows them to lead fulfilling lives and build genuine relationships. Be real. Be honest. Be fearless. Be yourself. Love yourself. The transformation can be awesome. I know because it helped me learn to read and write.

CHAPTER EIGHT

PULL OFF THE LABEL

When I was younger, my maternal grandparents, John and Marlene Boll, liked to host these super cool family gatherings at the Grosse Pointe Yacht Club on Lake St. Clair every summer. The purpose of the meeting was twofold: It was a great way to get the family together in the middle of the summer, and it was also a time for their grandchildren to flex and share what they had accomplished the previous year.

My grandparents grew up during the Great Depression and didn't have an opportunity to attend college. They were all about hard work and built a very successful business from the ground up. They made sure to instill those values in each of us eight grandchildren. Every year, they asked us to set goals for the next twelve months. Some years, they'd take us to lunch individually to discuss what we had accomplished. In other years, they hosted formal family meetings so everyone could spill the beans on what they'd done.

In the summer of 2007, after I'd spent five months working with Steve Tattum and the other teachers and tutors at the Denver Academy, I was sporting my fancy blue blazer and sweetest tie, and I couldn't wait to attend the family meeting. Why? I was so excited to drop the mic and tell everyone that I could read and write. That day, after everyone had taken a seat around a massive table in the Commodore's Room, my grandpa, Papi, stood and asked, "So, kids, what have you been proud of this year?"

I threw up my hand like a lightning bolt before anyone else. I was sitting to Papi's right, and he turned toward me and smiled.

"One of my goals this year was to learn to read, and I did!" I told everyone with a smile on my face as wide as Lake Michigan.

Much to my surprise, there was dead silence in the room after I let the cat out of the bag. Even my parents were floored because I hadn't let them know what I was going to say. Finally, one of my cousins, looking rather nervous, asked, "What?"

Suddenly, it hit me like a sledgehammer. My cousins, grandparents, aunts, and uncles hadn't known that I couldn't read and write. They were aware of my medical problems and knew that school was challenging for me, but they weren't aware of the details of my learning differences.

"Tell 'em, J," Dad said to me to boost my confidence.

"Well, you all know I went to a new school in the winter and spring in Denver, right?" I explained. "When I started there, I could barely make out words most kindergarteners know. Now, I can read at a fifth-grade level!"

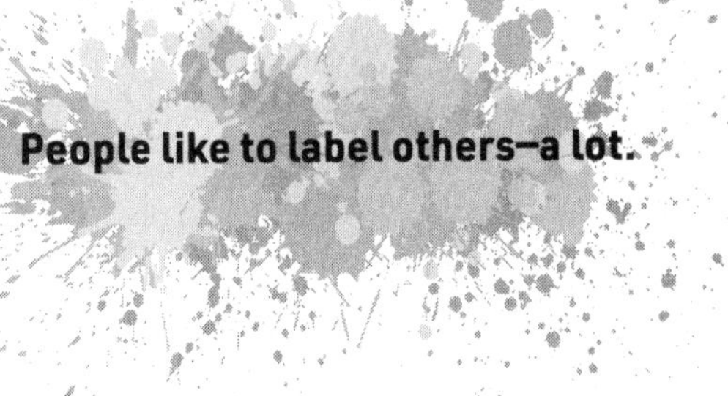

Later, Papi told my parents that he hadn't known the severity of my learning differences. He didn't want to admit it in front of the rest of his grandkids. "The truth of the matter is, all the cousins assumed he could read," Papi said.

My parents hadn't intentionally hidden anything from them. They were just always ones to focus on the positives and plow ahead. Besides, they didn't want others labeling me as illiterate or not smart, or something worse. They knew how mean kids can be.

People like to label others—a lot. We have labels for everything, based on a person's age, sex, ethnicity, political affiliation, religion, or where they live. It's like a national pastime in America. Labels like *Democrat*, *Republican*, *Southerner*, *Northerner*, *Christian*, *Atheist*, *African American*, *Caucasian*, and *Hispanic* aren't harmful. Those are descriptions we use to fit people into tidy groups to organize our lives.

It's the labels that people use to pass judgment on others they might not even know that are so hurtful. Those labels are based on assumptions and perceptions. They use those stereotypes to describe others. I'm sure you know what labels I'm talking about:

- Needy
- Slow
- Weird
- Loser
- Unattractive
- Useless
- Lazy
- Overweight
- Boring

You get the picture. How would you like to be labeled as someone who would never be able to read and write? That's what some of the teachers and administrators at University Liggett School said about me in the fifth grade. Looking back, I can't believe that adults would put such limits on a ten-year-old. They simply wanted to give up on me. They wanted my parents and me to stop fighting. They wanted to label me as a failure and illiterate, when I still had my entire life in front of me.

That's the lasting damage that labels can have. Fortunately, my parents refused to accept such a short-sighted assessment and never gave up on me. They continued to fight for me and found the best schools and tutors to help me. What about the other children with learning differences who might not have such supportive parents or the financial resources to go to a wonderful school like the Denver Academy? How much have the labels of being "dumb," a "failure," or an "under-achiever" held them back? How different would their lives have been?

Now, let me ask you this: Because of his dyslexia, what if legendary novelist F. Scott Fitzgerald had never learned to read? What if the American industrialist Henry Ford, who was dyslexic, had simply given up? Or what if teachers had given up on film director Steven Spielberg because of his learning differences? We never would have been able to read *The Great Gatsby*, drive a Ford F-150, or watch *Jurassic Park* or *Saving Private Ryan.*

There are so many people out there with learning differences whom others have unfairly labeled. According to the International Dyslexia Association, about one half of US students who qualify for special education are classified as having a learning disability. There are thirteen categories covered under the Individuals with Disabilities Education Act (IDEA), including attention deficit, autism, anxiety, depression, stuttering, and blindness. About 85 percent of those students have a learning difference in reading and language processing.

The International Dyslexia Association estimates that perhaps as much as 15 to 20 percent of the US population as a whole—an estimated 24 million people—have some form of dyslexia, "including slow or inaccurate reading, poor spelling, poor writing, or mixing up similar words."[25]

"Dyslexia occurs in people of all backgrounds and intellectual levels," the International Dyslexia Association website continues. "People with dyslexia can be very bright. They are often capable or even gifted in areas such as art, computer science, design, drama, electronics, math, mechanics, music, physics, sales, and sports."[26]

You won't believe the list of famous people who struggled in school and were diagnosed with dyslexia or other learning differences. They include inventors, scientists, political leaders, athletes, artists, actors and actresses, military heroes, journalists, filmmakers, and writers. Each one of them overcame adversity and impacted the world in remarkable ways. The list includes some of the greatest achievers in history:

- Mohammad Ali, heavyweight boxing champion
- Gwen Stefani, singer and judge on *The Voice*
- Albert Einstein, inventor

- Tom Holland, *Spider-Man* actor
- Jennifer Anniston, *Friends* actress
- Pablo Picasso, painter and sculptor
- Keanu Reeves, *Matrix* actor
- Chris Rock, comedian
- Tom Cruise, *Top Gun* actor

Tim Tebow won the Heisman Trophy as the best college football player in the country at the University Florida in 2007 and helped the Gators win two national championships. After college, he was an NFL quarterback and a professional baseball player with the New York Mets. Tim was diagnosed with dyslexia when he was seven years old.

Dyslexia runs in Tim's family; he told the *New York Post* about the condition during an interview in 2012. His father, Bob, and brother, Robby, are also dyslexic. His mother, Pamela, homeschooled Tim and his siblings.

Like me, Tim is a kinesthetic learner and learns best by completing tasks and writing lessons down, rather than reading textbooks or listening to lectures. Tim graduated from the University of Florida with a 3.7 GPA. He never let his learning differences stop him from becoming one of the most famous athletes in the world, who is as appreciated as much for his faith and kindness as his exploits on the football field and baseball diamond. He now works as a college football analyst for ESPN and the SEC Network.

"There's a lot of people that have certain processing disabilities and it has nothing to do with your intelligence, which I think is a big misconception that people have," Tim told the *Post*. "I've always tried to share, especially with kids, to be confident with it. You know, 'Hey, this isn't something that's a handicap. You just must learn how you learn and overcome it. It's something that you can be better off... because you know how you learn.'"[27]

What does Tim think about labeling people?

"When kids get labeled as a dyslexic, they think, 'Oh man, does this make me dumb?'" he said. "'Does this make me stupid? Does this make me not as intelligent as this person?' Absolutely not."[28]

One of the most amazing people I've met who overcame dyslexia is Kes Tomlin, who grew up in Georgetown, Ohio, during the 1970s. Back then, dyslexia was what Kes called a "buzzword" because nobody knew exactly how to diagnose it or treat it. It was kind of a catchall for learning disabilities. In kindergarten, Kes knew basic math but couldn't read the alphabet. Fortunately, he had a very strong-willed mother—sound familiar?—who was determined to help him learn to read and write. His mother pulled him out of classes one day and took him to a children's hospital in Cincinnati, Ohio, where he went through a battery of tests. Doctors diagnosed him with dyslexia and put together an individual learning plan to help him learn to read and write.

"When I read, I see a word and have to sound that word out," Kes said. "Once I get that word down, I've got to sound the next word out. I have to build the sentence and read the sentence once or twice before I can go on to the next sentence. So, I have to read a paragraph several times before I can really comprehend it."[29]

Kes's mother, Marsha Ann Tomlin, was a librarian and educator. She searched for a special school for him but

You just must learn how you learn and overcome it.

couldn't find one the family could afford. Administrators at his school said they didn't have the resources to accommodate his individual learning plan, so his mother found a different school that did. He switched districts and was placed in a learning disabilities classroom in the second grade.

That's where Kes met a teacher, Roger Cote, who helped change his life. Cote implemented the learning plan verbatim. Kes spent half the school day working on math and the other half learning to read. By the fourth grade, he was reading at a first-grade level. At the same time, he was taking eighth-grade courses in math and science. It was at that point that his teachers decided Kes needed to take regular classes, including social studies, earth science, and other subjects.

"That was a nightmare because it was a lot of reading," Kes said. "I'd come home, and my mom would read the books to me and help me with all of my writing. We worked every night until 11 o'clock trying to get my homework done. She was just dedicated to supporting me."

When Kes fell behind his classmates, his mother would come up with creative ways to motivate him. She instilled a relentless drive and ambition in him to succeed. Even though his eyesight wasn't affected, the Association of the Blind furnished him with audio books to help him learn.

In one class in middle school, Kes had to remember twenty-five facts about United States presidents. He worked hard to memorize the material. Here's how the test went down: Students could ask any other student a question. If students answered it correctly, they remained in the game. If they didn't, they had to sit down and were eliminated. There was another rule: Students couldn't ask someone back-to-back questions. But on the day of the test, Kes figured out that some of the students were plotting against him by asking him every other question to eliminate him.

For whatever reason, there was one girl in the class who didn't understand why Kes was taking special classes and why he didn't have to take spelling tests like everyone else. So, when Kes made it to the finals with another student, she asked him to spell America. He had been studying the names and facts surrounding presidents—not how to spell the name of our country. Still, he nailed it. Then the girl pointed out that he had failed to say "capital A" when he started. He was eliminated and finished second. It wasn't the only time he had to stand up for himself.

"I stood on my own and they quit trying to mess with me," Kes said. "I'm glad that I could defend myself. It just taught me to be a role model. It taught me to respect others. It taught me to appreciate people that were different from me because I was very different from anybody else."[30]

In middle school, Kes found another fierce advocate in Debbie Mowers, who worked with other teachers to tailor their lesson plans to fit his needs. Kes found subjects that interested him and didn't require as much reading. As a freshman, he completed a physics problem that proved Newton's third law of motion and advanced all the way to the state level in a science fair. His father had woodworking tools in the garage, so he went to shop class instead of study hall. That led to him working with a textbook author who was trying to bring technology to shop classes. Kes started building robots in the early eighties—and he was paid for it. He designed one of his robots from a potato chip can and broken toy. He learned how to write computer software on a Commodore 64 (ask your parents).

By the time Kes graduated from high school, he had traveled to the Bahamas, Hawaii, Iceland, Luxembourg, Germany, France, and Switzerland with a Christian mission group. He graduated third in his senior class after completing four quarters of college courses. He chose to attend Wright State University

What I've learned in my life, perhaps more than anything else, is that labels are for jars—not people.

in Dayton, Ohio, in part because of its reputation of accommodating students with learning differences. He received a full presidential scholarship and enrolled in the honors program.

At Wayne State, the robotics teacher tracked Kes down after reading about the robots he'd built in high school. He ended up working closely with the professor, developing a conveyor belt with optical character recognition and another robot that took items off the belt. He graduated from college with a 3.6 GPA. He interviewed with the US Department of Defense, landed a job, and went to work in Washington, DC.

In the beginning, Kes thought he would work for the federal government for three or four years to gain some experience. His career has now spanned more than three decades at the Naval Surface Warfare Center, Carderock Division in Bethesda, Maryland. He is the branch head of a system development group that does onboard submarine acoustic trials. In short, Kes and his team soundproof submarines so foreign enemies can't detect them under water. He also works with subs from the Royal Navy of the United Kingdom and the Royal Australian Navy.

That's right, the boy who couldn't read is now a research scientist working on submarines. Looking back at his life, Kes credits his mother and wife for helping him shed the labels that are often associated with dyslexia and other learning differences. He met Lisa Adams when he was twelve years old. She helped him with reading and writing; he helped her with math and science. She joined him at Wright State. They married while in college and have been together ever since.

Like Tim Tebow and so many others, Kes refused to give in to his learning differences. When we're faced with challenges or obstacles in life, we build amazing qualities like perseverance, stamina, grit, and self-belief. I firmly believe that if you go through life without obstacles, you're going to coast and not accomplish anything meaningful. People like Tim and Kes didn't believe the superficial labels others tried to place on them.

What I've learned in my life, perhaps more than anything else, is that labels are for jars—not people. Have you ever tried to remove one of those annoying labels off an item you purchased on Amazon or a Christmas gift you unwrapped? As soon as you start peeling, it tears apart and leaves half the label and, worse, sticky glue on the gift. Most of the time, you can't peel it off with your fingernails or scrub it off with a rag. Even after you soak it in soapy hot water, there's still unsightly residue left behind. It's the worst!

Now imagine how someone feels when he or she has been labeled. They can't peel off what others might say about them. The painful words can't be undone or scrubbed away. Instead of using labels to demean people or bring them down, let's pick words that inspire them to reach their fullest potential and encourage them to be authentic and original—to be themselves. If we must use labels, let's choose the good ones like:

- Kind
- Honest
- Considerate
- Confident
- Smart
- Funny
- Optimistic
- Curious

- Loyal
- Loving
- Hardworking
- Interesting
- Genuine

More than anything else, remember that your words carry weight. As Proverbs 18:21 says: "The tongue has the power of life and death, and those who love it will eat its fruit." We must choose our words carefully and be slow to speak. We must think about how our words will make others feel.

I still believe labels should be left to jars and clothes. If we must use them, our tongues should choose words that build others up, not ones that tear others down. Think before you speak. Be thoughtful. Be kind.

CHAPTER NINE

STRETCH YOURSELF

EVEN THOUGH I'VE FACED SEVERAL MEDICAL CHALLENGES throughout my life, I've always been a bit of a daredevil. I love challenging myself with thrilling adventures, sometimes to the extreme and often in the great outdoors. Whether it's flying down a steep trail on a mountain bike, shredding through a powder-covered trail in the Rockies on a pair of skis, or carefully trekking up one of the tallest peaks in the world, the untamed wilderness is where I've felt the most alive and closest to God.

Now, I must admit that my mother isn't the biggest fan of my thrill seeking. She values safety and security in my life but has slowly come to terms with danger following me around like a shadow at times.

Here's the perfect example: In August 2010, my parents and I traveled to Zimbabwe with some family friends. The land-locked country of about 15.5 million people is located northeast of South Africa. Its breathtaking savannas are home to lions, leopards, cheetahs, jackals, elephants, giraffes, hippopotamuses, and rhinoceroses.

Another unforgettable sight is Victoria Falls, which is located on the western border, between Zambia and Zimbabwe. With a combined width of 5,604 feet and

The untamed wilderness is where I've felt the most alive and closest to God.

height of 354 feet, Victoria Falls is recognized as the largest waterfall in the world. The Kololo people who once lived in the area described it as "The Smoke that Thunders" because of the immense spray and booming roar the sheets of water make when falling over the edge. Victoria Falls is roughly twice as wide and two times as tall as Niagara Falls.

We traveled to Victoria Falls not only to see God's magnificent creation, but also because some of our family friends had decided to bungee jump from the Victoria

Falls Bridge, a border crossing point between Zimbabwe and Zambia. Of course, I knew my friends weren't going to take the frightening plunge without me—but I had to convince my parents that it was safe for me to do it first!

As we walked across the bridge and saw the mighty Zambezi River more than 350 feet below us, Mom asked Dad, "You're not going to let him do it, right?" She was concerned about me jumping from the bridge for more than one reason. Not only was it extremely dangerous to be dropped above a crocodile-infested river, but I'd also undergone a risky surgery only five years earlier.

Back in the fall of 2005, only a few weeks after the school psychologist gave my parents the difficult news that I was going to struggle with reading and writing for the rest of my life, I faced one of my greatest medical challenges.

It was my first season playing football for the Grosse Pointe Red Barons. I might have been one of the smaller ten-year-olds on the field, but that didn't stop my coach, Tony Cimmarrusti, from playing me at center, slap in the middle of the trenches. I was tough for my size and didn't complain much about the physical nature of the sport because, let's face it, I'd dealt with pain and being uncomfortable for most of my life.

But I was keeping a secret from my parents: My legs and back often hurt after practices and games. It became more difficult to conceal my pain when my neck started twitching, almost like I had Tourette's syndrome.

I didn't tell my parents or anyone else because I feared they would make me stop playing.

Finally, during one of our games near the end of the season, I couldn't bear the pain any longer. After a series of plays, I hobbled off the field to our bench. Mom and Dad came down from the metal bleachers to check on me.

"Hey, J, did you get hurt?" Dad asked me.

"No, Dad, I've been hurting for a while now, on and off," I confessed.

Mom had a concerned look on her face. She knew I had a high pain tolerance and that I often didn't tell them when I was hurting.

When we got home, Mom called my pediatrician, Dr. Douglas Ziegler. I knew what that meant: more tests and who knew what else. When we arrived at Dr. Ziegler's office the next day, he told me to walk to the nurse's desk and back. I walked up the hallway, trying not to limp. My body tingled with discomfort and my neck was stiff. I could barely bend over and touch my toes.

Initially, Dr. Ziegler ordered an X-ray and saw nothing wrong. Then, he ordered blood tests, which didn't turn up any red flags. He told my parents to keep an eye on me and sent us home. Only a few days later, however, Dr. Ziegler woke up in the middle of the night worried about me. He sent me for an MRI just to make certain there wasn't something serious going on.

I had an MRI on January 27, 2006. After Dr. Ziegler and other physicians read my results, they gave me a diagnosis: tethered spinal cord syndrome. Of course, I was too young back then to know what having a tethered spinal cord meant. As it turned out, my parents were all too familiar with the scary condition. There's a high rate of tethered spinal cord syndrome in people with VATER association, especially if they've had an imperforate anus like me. Because I was at greater risk, my parents had kept a close eye on me over the years, looking for symptoms.

As a child, I had severe headaches, which led to many MRIs to make sure my spinal cord wasn't tethered. Thankfully, each one came back clean. I'd had back pain over the years as well, but going to the chiropractor, stretching, and massages usually made it go away.

Tethered spinal cord syndrome wasn't good news, and there was a chance my condition might get much worse. Here's what happens: When fibers from the spinal cord become attached (or tethered) to tissue around the spine, the cord is stretched—and damaged—as the spine grows. In many ways, a tethered spinal cord is like a tightly stretched rubber band—or a bungee cord. If you put a rubber band under extreme pressure for an extended period, it's going to snap. Scar tissue can develop and restrict the flow of fluids, and cysts can form and lead to a loss of movement, chronic pain, trouble walking, and even permanent paralysis.

This was serious.

Immediately, doctors told me that I had to stop playing sports. No more football. No more lacrosse. It wasn't the news a sports-loving ten-year-old boy wanted to hear. Remember what I said about being flexible? Once again, life—and the good Lord—gave me lemons, so I made lemonade. I became a manager with the lacrosse team the next spring and learned to enjoy the game that way, cheering my friends and teammates all season long.

Dr. Ziegler told my parents to find a pediatric neurosurgeon as quickly as possible. Mom and Dad had a consultation with a neurosurgeon at Children's Hospital of Michigan. They wanted a second opinion, so they called my surgeon, Dr. Alberto Peña, who by then had moved to Cincinnati Children's Hospital. He recommended Dr. Kerry Crone, one of his fellow surgeons there. Mom and Dad sent Dr. Crone my medical records and MRI images, and we left for a short trip to my grandparents' winter home in Key Largo, Florida.

During the flight to the Florida Keys, pain shot up and down my lower back and leg. That night, I lost control of my bladder and had an accident in bed, which hadn't happened in a very long time. Mom and Dad didn't tell me at the time, but the loss of bowel and bladder control is a sign that tethered spinal cord syndrome is becoming more serious.

The next morning, Mom called Dr. Crone's office and described my worsening symptoms to one of his nurses. I went offshore fishing with Dad and a couple of others.

By the time Dr. Crone called Mom back, we were five miles offshore—with three sixty- to eighty-pound sailfish set on lines! We had a triple-on!

After asking Mom a few questions about my symptoms, Dr. Crone said, "What you are describing to me is nerve damage. JT's tethered cord is causing him a possibly irreversible situation. He needs surgery ASAP. Where are you?"

Mom let him know we were in the Florida Keys.

Once again, life—and the good Lord—gave me lemons, so I made lemonade.

"Mrs. Mestdagh," Dr. Crone said with a very serious tone in his voice, "you need to do whatever you can to get to Cincinnati as soon as possible. It's absolutely essential."

After hanging up the phone, Mom sat down and tried to collect her thoughts. She couldn't help but cry. Mom took a few breaths and called Dad's cell phone. "JT has to get to Cincinnati Children's Hospital now. His tethered cord has become very bad!"

Dad couldn't hear her well because of the roaring engines. Plus, we had three monster fish on hooks! It was absolute chaos on deck. Dad waited until I landed my fish, took a few photographs, and then released it back into the blue water. Then he called Mom back and heard the scary update. We headed back to shore—and I didn't know exactly why. That night, after a wonderful dinner, my parents broke the news that I had to get to Cincinnati for surgery as soon as possible.

On February 20, 2006, we met with Dr. Crone and another surgeon who were going to perform the procedure. Dr. Crone said my tethered cord was low in my spine and extremely tight. The good news was that he was confident he could release it by going through the vertebrae, rather than taking them out.

As I waited in my hospital room for the surgery the next day, our family friend, Grace Fenton, prayed with me and hugged me. So did Mom and Dad. I took deep breaths so I wouldn't cry. I knew there was a possibility that I could wake up paralyzed and never walk again.

The surgery lasted three hours. Dr. Crone made an incision in my lower back and removed tiny portions of the wings of my L4 and L5 vertebrae in the lumbar region, right above the sacrum. Then, he gently opened the dura mater, the thick membrane protecting my spinal cord, and searched for exactly where my spinal cord was attached. With an extremely steady hand, he released the cord successfully.

Dr. Crone finally walked out of the operating room around 6 p.m. He told Mom and Dad that the procedure had gone exactly as he had hoped. I was awake and could feel my legs and toes. I would be walking better soon, Dr. Crone promised, and my back and neck pain would be gone. Dr. Crone told my parents that when he released my tethered spinal cord, "it literally shot up, like a rubber band!"

By the next day, I was showing signs of improvement and acting more like myself. Physical therapy was painful and I couldn't do much the first couple days. In fact, it took me forty minutes to get out of bed the first time (yes, forty minutes!). But eventually, Dr. Crone's promise came true—my pain was gone and I was able to go back to snow skiing, hiking, and some of my other favorite physical activities.

Which brings me back to August 2010, when I was standing on Victoria Falls Bridge, about a month before I was scheduled to start my freshman year of high school. When Mom voiced concerns about me taking the plunge, Dad assured her that the people in charge wouldn't allow me to jump.

"He can't do it," Dad assured her. "He won't meet the age requirement. He won't even meet the weight requirement. There's no way they'll let him jump."

But when I walked up to the ticket window and told the man that I wanted to jump, he replied, "OK, where's your money?" I didn't meet the minimum age (fourteen years) or weight (about eighty-eight pounds), but no one in charge questioned me. Mom almost fainted right then and there.

After reassuring her that everything was going to be fine, I stepped out on the small steel platform. Two men attached ankle and body harnesses to me. They did a couple of safety checks. One man asked if I was ready. I spread my arms, as if I was going to soar into the sky like an eagle. My heart was racing. The man counted down: "Five, four, three, two . . . " And then, all of a sudden, he pushed me and screamed, "Bungee!"

The freefall lasted only four seconds, but it was one of the most thrilling moments of my life. The backdrop of Victoria Falls and the Zambezi River was awe-inspiring. Just before it seemed like I might crash into the rocks of the Bakota Gorge, I was rescued by a gut-wrenching jerk. I don't think Mom and Dad started breathing again until I stopped bouncing, grabbed the cord, and gave them a big smile and thumbs up. Soon, a man was unhooking me from the bungee cord and latching me onto his line. I was back on dry land in a couple of minutes.

Now, imagine my parents' horror when they learned that, a little over a year later, a twenty-two-year-old Australian tourist making the same jump plunged into the Zambezi River when the cord snapped in two. Erin Langworthy jumped on New Year's Eve 2012. She had to swim to shore with her feet tied and free the cord when it became entangled in rocks. Miraculously, she suffered only cuts, bruises, and a broken collarbone. No more bungee jumping for me!

But this bungee jump wasn't the only way I was stretched that year. My first year of high school was also my first year back at University Liggett School, where their new headmaster, Dr. Joseph P. Healey, welcomed me with open arms. It was going well. Some kids might not have accepted the challenge of going back to a place where they were previously not wanted, but not me. I looked forward to paving the way for kids with learning differences in the new program, to make it better for those who might end up there in the future. I wasn't afraid to stretch myself–even if the first few weeks might have been uncomfortable.

While things were good in school and at home, once again my body had other ideas. In February 2011, I started experiencing severe back pain again. I constantly cracked my neck and back to relieve pain and stiffness and asked my parents for back rubs. I rolled on a Styrofoam roller on the floor to help alleviate the pain and tried hanging upside down. Nothing seemed to work. Things in the plumbing department weren't good either. We weren't sure what was going on.

At Cincinnati Children's Hospital, I had a scoliosis X-ray and an abdominal X-ray, as well as a test that measured how efficiently my bladder emptied. Next, I had an appointment with Dr. Crone, who had overseen my tethered cord surgery five years earlier. Dr. Crone had seen an MRI from a Detroit hospital, didn't like it, and worried something might be wrong. He ordered another MRI with me lying on my stomach.

Early the next morning, we returned to Dr. Crone's office. He was unavailable so we met with Mimi, his nurse. She showed us the scan. Right away, we could see what was wrong. I started to choke up. Mom's eyes watered. Dad swallowed hard.

My spinal cord was tethered again.

We left the office and wandered into the long hallway. I stared out the window at the Cincinnati skyline. I was trying to hold back tears, but my head was about to explode. Finally, I let it out. I'd had more than a dozen surgeries by then, but none had been as painful as the one on my spine. The first time, my body hurt from head to toe. No recovery had been more difficult or lasted so long. I knew this time might be even worse because I was five years older. Once I came to grips with the situation, I leaned my shoulder against the cold window and sobbed. I could hear my parents crying behind me too.

Dad took me into the restroom. I splashed my face with water.

"We're going to take it one day at a time," he told me. "We'll get through this."

Re-tethering of the spinal cord occurs in up to 25 percent of patients with tethered spinal cord syndrome, according to the National Institutes of Health, although some studies have suggested it occurs in only 5 percent.

Either way, it's rare and I was on the wrong side of the statistics. Once again, I faced the terrifying possibility of becoming paralyzed.

About a month later, I returned to Cincinnati Children's Hospital for the surgery. When Dr. Crone opened my spinal column for the second time, he couldn't believe what he saw. I had two spots of tethering–one at the original spot and another slightly below it. He had never seen that before. Once again, God was with me, and I could feel His presence. The surgery was a success.

When I woke up, I was suffering from severe back spasms. The pain medication made me sick, and I was throwing up left and right. Two days after the surgery, Dad ordered me out of bed to walk. The recovery was as bad as I feared it would be. But eventually, I was able to go home and begin my rehabilitation.

Since my recovery would last a while, the administrators at University Liggett School agreed to let my final grades be what they were when I left for the hospital. I made up a few assignments and tests that summer, and overall, my freshman year was a success.

On June 13, 2011, I returned to school for Class Day, an end-of-the-year awards celebration. I sat in my chair and clapped for my classmates. Given my academic situation, I had no expectation of hearing my name called.

One of the final awards was the TiJuan Kidd Prize, which is named after a sophomore who was tragically killed in the summer of 1987. The prize is awarded annually to a freshman "who, with positive contagious energy, exemplifies the qualities TiJuan possessed: honesty, determination, confidence, and dependability."

When Dr. Healey called my name, I was completely surprised. My parents had stunned looks and wide smiles on their faces too. I walked to the stage, and I still remember my classmates clapping for me. Everything I had endured that year—the pain, anxiety, fear, and worry of the unknown—was gone.

God knows your full potential, and He doesn't want you settling for anything less.

How far have you stretched yourself? Are you reaching your full potential? Or are you only settling for mediocrity and the status quo? Stretching yourself requires a change and that's uncomfortable for many. Believe me, I know. However, when you stretch yourself and reach for the seemingly impossible, God steps in and makes the unimaginable possible. God knows your full potential, and He doesn't want you settling for anything less. Stretch yourself. Take chances. Be versatile like a rubber band. And remember to be kind to others. That's the greatest legacy one can have.

Back then, I couldn't have known that it wouldn't be the last time doctors would tell me I might have to change my lifestyle dramatically—and that my faith would be stretched.

CHAPTER TEN

WALK IN SOMEBODY ELSE'S SHOES

HOW MANY TIMES HAVE YOU HAD THAT "IF I HAD only listened" moment? Like when you were on your phone rather than doing your chores, which caused your parents to discipline you, so you missed a party. Or when you didn't follow a teacher's instructions before completing a project, so you had to do it all over again.

When you take time to listen to others, you'll learn something about someone else, and you'll probably discover something about yourself too. Listening is like having a superpower, and you'll transform into Iron Man or Wonder Woman if you use it. Remember the old saying about God giving us two ears and only one mouth? He wants us to listen twice as much as we're talking. He wants us to listen to others—and Him.

Before we rush to judge someone else, we need to understand where he or she is coming from. We need to listen to their story and walk in their shoes to truly understand them. We need to walk beside them long enough, so our shoes begin to feel like theirs.

I'm certain of one thing: I'm glad others listened to me—and walked in my shoes—in my greatest times of need, and that God listened to my prayers.

During my junior year at University Liggett School,

We need to walk beside them long enough, so our shoes begin to feel like theirs.

I began to seriously think about where I would attend college. It hadn't been that long ago that going to college seemed like a far-fetched dream for me. Since I was doing well in school and my grades were good, I decided that I wouldn't limit myself. I was going to apply to a handful of Ivy League schools, including Princeton University, and I wasn't going to sell myself short.

The director of college guidance, on the other hand, had ideas of her own. When we had a meeting to discuss my potential college choices, her list didn't include Ivy League institutions. When I asked her why, she said, "Why waste your time, JT?"

Thankfully, another counselor, Beth Beckmann, could see the full potential in me. She told me about one of her former students, a young man named Forrest. There was a photograph of him on her desk. When I asked about Forrest, she said, "At my school in New York, we took in a seventh grader who also had learning issues. I kind of shepherded him through. He ended up at Princeton." That's when the lightbulb went off for me. I went home and told my parents that I wanted to be the "Forrest of Liggett."

I knew getting into a college that I liked was going to be an uphill climb. Not every school out there has programs for students with learning differences, and that was a top priority. Yet, in my heart, I knew I'd worked too hard to lower my expectations. With help and dedication from a lot of kind people, I'd put myself in a position to graduate from high school with a killer GPA.

I kept working with Steve Tattum whenever he was in Michigan, typically four times a year, and I tagged along when he trained teachers in the state. I was happy to share my progress and experiences in the F.A.S.T. Reading System.

Over time, though, I figured out how to be my own advocate. I asked teachers for help when I needed it and fought for accommodations when I thought they were necessary. I wasn't shy about standing up for myself.

That summer, my parents and I hopped a plane to North Carolina to tour a trio of colleges that I had interest in: Elon University, Guilford College, and High Point University. I was also thinking about Curry College in Milton, Massachusetts, the first university in the country to provide academic assistance to students with learning differences.

We knew very little about High Point, just that it was a liberal arts college established in 1924, and is affiliated with the United Methodist Church. It is located in the Piedmont Triad region of North Carolina, about ninety miles west of Raleigh. We didn't have any family or friends who had gone to High Point. No one from University Liggett had ever attended college there, so my teachers and counselors were just as unfamiliar with it as we were.

The day before my official college tours, Dad had a great idea to kill time–we'd drive to each of the campuses and get to know our way around. High Point was our last pit stop of the day. When we pulled onto campus, there was a flashing purple LED sign in a parking space reserved for special guests. My name was in lights, just like on Broadway:

JT MESTDAGH
UNIVERSITY LIGGETT
GROSSE POINTE, MI

We climbed out of our rental car and strolled around campus. It was beautifully manicured with massive brick buildings. I could hear faint classical music coming from somewhere. I'm not kidding, I felt like Kevin Costner in *Field of Dreams. Is this heaven? No, it's North Carolina,* I thought to myself.

The moment I stepped out of the rental car, I knew High Point was the place where I could spend the next four years. Dad suggested we find the Phillips School of Business, since I was interested in majoring in a subject related to that field. We located the impressive two-story structure with four giant white columns. We stepped inside, and everything was new and stylish.

We headed back to the promenade, a wide central greenway lined with flags from across the globe. I'm telling you, everything about the campus was perfect. I was more than certain that I wanted to be a student at High Point after only a few minutes on campus. "I'm going here," I whispered to myself.

Just then, the doors to Hayworth Chapel swung open, and students with wide smiles started making their way down the steps. High Point holds chapel service every Wednesday at 5:30 p.m., and the service was just wrapping up. As we watched the students pour out, a distinguished-looking man walked among the students, smiling and chatting. Dad recognized him. It was Dr. Nido R. Qubein, the president of High Point University.

President Qubein noticed us, a family he knew nothing about, and he walked over and introduced himself. President Qubein was a very successful entrepreneur, businessman, and consultant before moving into higher education. And let me tell you, he is a master of personal communication. He has written books about communicating effectively, given thousands of motivational speeches, and consulted with many Fortune 500 companies. After only a few minutes, it was easy to see why. He asked about my aspirations and goals and even complimented the red driving shoes that Dad and I were wearing. He listened closely and made me feel like no one else was on campus at that moment, like all great leaders do.

When I told Mom and Dad that I wanted to go to school there, Mom's heart sank. She thought the odds of High Point accepting me were stacked against me. She didn't want me to be disappointed. Deep down, I knew that's where I was supposed to go. It was just a feeling that I had, like a tap on the shoulder from the Holy Spirit.

Three weeks later, my acceptance letter arrived from High Point University. It was one of the happiest days of my life. President Qubein could appreciate the health problems, learning differences, and other obstacles I had overcome throughout my life. He was a brilliant man and had his health, yet he had overcome so much as a child. After High Point accepted me, Dad sent President Qubein his own pair of the red driving shoes we were wearing on campus. Then, he could truly walk in my shoes.

President Nido Qubein was born in Lebanon. His father became ill when Nido was only three years old. His father died when Nido was six, leaving his wife, Victoria, to care for her three sons and two daughters. Nido's mother had only a fourth-grade education, but she was blessed with a wealth of knowledge and worked very hard to support her family.

He listened closely and made me feel like no one else was on campus at that moment, like all great leaders do.

When President Qubein was young, his mother told him, "To be a great person, walk hand in hand and side by side with great people."[31] He took his mother's advice to heart and surrounded himself with great people who would help him be successful. When President Qubein was seventeen years old, his mother encouraged him to go to the United States to study. He arrived here with fifty dollars in his pocket. He could speak very little

English. He taught himself to speak the native language by learning five new words every day.

Shortly after moving to North Carolina, President Qubein convinced the admissions folks at Mount Olive College to accept him as an international student. He excelled in his classes, while working for the school and at YMCA summer camps. One of the turning points in President Qubein's life happened during his sophomore year. He saved $375 to purchase an automobile, but the cheapest car he could find was $750. President Qubein told his housemother, Verta Lawhon, about his problem. She was a retired teacher, receiving about $100 in Social Security benefits and $100 in salary from the college every month.

At the end of the month, President Qubein checked his bank balance and was surprised to see $750 in his account. At first, he believed the bank made an error, but then it hit him: Mrs. Lawhon had doubled his balance by dipping into whatever savings she had. She had listened to his needs and decided to make a real difference in his life. That remarkable gesture of kindness left quite an impression on President Qubein and provided him with a lesson he would never forget: It is better to give than to receive.

Then, there was another incident that hit President Qubein like a two-by-four across the head. Shortly before President Qubein left Mount Olive, the university president told him that even though he had been working ten hours a day, his wages hadn't been enough to pay what he owed in tuition, room, and board. In fact, there was a sizable balance on his account. Fortunately, a doctor in a neighboring town had already paid for it. President Qubein was so moved by the doctor's kind gesture that he wanted to meet him and personally thank him. But the doctor wanted to remain anonymous, and President Qubein has never known his identity to this day.

President Qubein earned his associate degree in business from Mount Olive, a bachelor's degree in human relations from High Point University in 1970, and a Master of Science in business education from the University of North Carolina-Greensboro in 1973. All these years later, President Qubein knows his academic career would have never happened without the kindness of Mrs. Lawhon, and the generosity of the doctor. If they hadn't listened to the inspiring story of the international student who had worked so hard to achieve the American dream, he might have never been able to finish school.

When President Qubein left graduate school, he had $500 in the bank and launched a company that supplied leadership materials for adults working with children at schools, churches, and summer camps. Before too long, he had more than six thousand customers in thirty countries. President Qubein followed through on his promise to God. By 2001, he had given more than five hundred scholarships worth $2 million—and many, many more since—to students attending Mount Olive, High Point, and UNC-Greensboro.

You'd be surprised by how much you can help others just by listening to their stories. After my first book, *No Bad Days*, was published, the mother of a young man in Grand Rapids, Michigan, reached out to my family. Her son, Matthew Olson, had been through a rough stretch—the kind of medical problems no one should have to endure. Matthew's problems started in high school. He broke his back playing football as a junior, and it took doctors a while to figure out the correct diagnosis: fractures of his L4 and L5 vertebrae. That required two surgeries and wearing an uncomfortable clamshell brace for the better part of a year.

Once Matthew recovered, he got a scholarship to play lacrosse at Hope College in Holland, Michigan. Then he tore the ACL in his knee and had another surgery. This is when things got bad: The incision site on his knee became infected, and (long story short) he ended up with an infection in his colon, which means they had to remove a sizable section of his large intestine.

In 2022, Matthew and his family started working with a highly regarded specialist at Johns Hopkins Hospital in Baltimore, Maryland. She discovered that food was passing through his small and large intestine fine, but nothing was getting through his colon. Doctors tried to fix things through medicine and physical therapy, but nothing would work. So, in

September 2022, Matthew had a total colectomy, in which surgeons removed the rest of his large intestine. He went from going to the bathroom about once every two or three weeks to thirty to forty times a day. While it was a difficult way to live, Matthew was at least happy that he was no longer in pain.

That all changed in December 2022. Matthew woke up one morning and had extreme discomfort in his stomach. He started vomiting. His then-girlfriend was at work. His friends weren't answering their phones. No one was around to help him, so Matthew drove himself to the hospital. An MRI at the emergency room revealed an obstruction in his small intestine. He had emergency surgery to remove the blockage. Unfortunately, a surgeon nicked his small intestine in four places during the procedure. The doctors didn't realize it and sewed him back up. Three days after the surgery, when Matthew got up to walk for the first time, his stomach ruptured because there was so much pressure from his small intestine leaking. He had another emergency surgery, but doctors couldn't find the leaks. They cleaned him out and sewed him back up.

Within hours of the second surgery, Matthew was septic. He had lost twenty pounds. Doctors took him back into the operating room to try to find the leak and save his life. They couldn't find it. Doctors told Matthew's parents that he wasn't improving and that they were out of ideas.

"They told my parents to expect me not to come home from this and kind of say your goodbyes kind of thing because I was just crashing," Matthew said. "It wasn't good."[32]

On Christmas Eve, a different surgeon operated on Matthew one more time. It was his fourth surgery in a month. The new surgeon couldn't find the leak either, so he decided to perform an ileostomy. It's similar to a colostomy, where your waste is collected in a bag outside your body. The surgeon told Matthew that if his body healed well enough, there was a chance the ileostomy could be reversed after several months. When Matthew left the hospital, he had lost about forty pounds. He had an incision from his sternum to his pubic area.

While dealing with the loss of his grandfather, Matthew was still battling medical problems like a new leak in his small intestine, dehydration, and multiple infections. Finally, in June 2023, Matthew was well enough that doctors were able to reverse the ileostomy successfully.

Stunningly, this is when Matthew came closest to death. He had developed such a tolerance to pain medications that he required a crazy number of painkillers. While he was recovering from the ileostomy, a nurse gave him another dose but failed to check his vitals. When his mother, Laura, and his sister, Emily, walked into his hospital room, he was blue and cold. Matthew wasn't breathing. He didn't have a heartbeat or pulse.

They screamed for nurses, who gave Matthew twelve doses of Narcan to bring him back.

"When I woke up from that, I was so disoriented, I had no idea what had happened," Matthew said. "I woke up completely naked, surrounded by seventy people, all screaming and shouting and super concerned. You could feel that tension. I had no idea what had happened. And I looked in the corner, I could see my mom and sister, they're just bawling."

Thankfully, Matthew was able to recover, but his physical problems took an emotional toll on him. He had to defer medical school twice. His longtime girlfriend decided his situation was too much to handle. He ended up losing both of his grandfathers within a couple of months. Before Matthew's illness, he was very active and worked out. Exercise was the way he released stress and anxiety.

"It's like my antidepressant," Matthew said. "Having that taken away was extremely challenging. And not being able to go to med school or not being able to advance in a career, dealing with all these issues, constantly having setbacks and being in the hospital and just having such a terrible quality of life, it really got to me. My depression got really bad; my anxiety got really bad. And there were times I was like, 'Why me? I don't even want to continue.'"

When Matthew's mother reached out to my family, fate would have it that I was speaking at a place close to where he lives in northern Michigan. We ended up meeting and discovered that we both loved being outdoors, whether it's biking, boating, snowboarding, or hiking. Although our medical histories are different, I've experienced many of the same challenges, both mentally and physically, as him. I've walked in his shoes. In fact, I've run a marathon in them. I listened to his story and encouraged him to focus on his small victories and not worry as much about the big picture. I'm happy to report

Choose your words carefully and take time to listen.

that Matthew is doing much better. He'll be attending medical school soon.

Listen to other people's stories. It's the only way you're going to figure out what someone is really going through, and it allows them to feel heard and understood. Walk in their shoes. Always listen intently to others and ask someone how he or she feels. You might be surprised by their answer. If you don't listen to others, you won't know how you can help and inspire them, which is the greatest gift we can give. Choose your words carefully and take time to listen. The sincerest form of respect is taking the time to truly listen to someone.

With all the modern technology that we have for communicating with each other even across the world, it seems that most people have forgotten how to communicate clearly with someone who's standing right next to them. Listening has become a lost art. That's too bad because knowing how to listen effectively can bring you a lot of benefits. It can strengthen both personal and professional relationships.

Remember, others won't always be able to recall everything you say in a conversation, but they'll likely remember how you made them feel. Stop and listen. It's the kind thing to do. If you don't listen to others, you won't know how you can help and inspire them. You won't know how many lives you can change.

CHAPTER ELEVEN

GET SOME GREEN TIME

THERE'S LITTLE QUESTION THAT SOCIAL MEDIA HAS become an integral part of our daily lives in today's world. It helps us stay connected with family, friends, and people around the globe. We can watch millions of funny videos about cats and dogs, and we can learn just about anything with a few swipes of our thumbs. Social media is also a great place to raise support for a cause that's dear to our hearts, or to find empathy or a good laugh with friends if we're having a bad day.

Of course, like just about anything else in life, too much of something might not be good for the soul (or the belly). If you eat an entire bag of Oreos in one sitting, instead of one or two cookies, you're probably not going to feel very good. Downing a twelve-pack of Red Bulls in one afternoon will probably leave you bouncing off the walls (or in the hospital). How much time you spend on social media is no different.

Dr. Nusheen Ameenuddin, a pediatrician at the Mayo Clinic, believes social media becomes a problem for teenagers and young adults when the time they're spending on TikTok, Instagram, and other apps replaces sleep, physical activities, and face-to-face communication with family and friends.

"What we've learned in the past ten to fifteen years is

Of course, like just about anything else in life, too much of something might not be good for the soul (or the belly).

that some kids are going to be more susceptible to depression and other mental health problems than others," Dr. Ameenuddin said. "But it's not true of every kid."[33]

Dr. Ameenuddin explained that the prefrontal cortex of a teenager's brain hasn't fully developed. That's the area of the brain that controls impulsive behavior. It's more difficult for teenagers to stop a habit that might harm them or influence them to make bad decisions.

Teens might *know* they shouldn't be spending so much time on social media, but their brains aren't developed enough to make them put down their phones or shut their laptops. The companies behind the social media apps aren't doing enough to stop addictive behaviors, either. They want us scrolling and clicking on everything because that's how they make money—and they make a lot of it.

"The algorithms aren't designed with kids' brains or development in mind," Dr. Ameenuddin said. "They're designed to keep kids scrolling and clicking for ongoing engagement, regardless of quality, accuracy, or safety of the content itself." [34]

Chris R. Mazzarella, a psychologist and executive coach at Heritage Professional Associates in Wheaton, Illinois, has spent nearly three decades helping teenagers and young adults. He has worked in hospitals, in-patient units, outpatient facilities, and schools. The patients he is counseling and coaching now are much different than the ones he worked with at the start of his career.

"In my sessions with patients and their parents, they're referencing a world in which they're constantly on a screen, digesting images and content, and they're being shaped in terms of how they see themselves, how they see their friends, whether or not they think that they have a place in this world," Mazzarella said. "So, all of it is influenced by what's going on on the Internet, these videos that they see every day. I don't think I've really met a young person in the last fifteen years that hasn't been significantly shaped by the content that they're taking in."[35]

Surveys show that today's teens are digesting social media like never before. A 2022 study by the Pew Research Center found that many teens use popular social media sites like YouTube, TikTok, Instagram, and Snapchat. The survey of 1,316 teenagers aged thirteen to seventeen years found that 95 percent were active on YouTube, 62 percent used Instagram, and 59 percent spent time on Snapchat. They reported using apps like Twitter (23 percent), Twitch (20 percent), WhatsApp (1 percent), Reddit (14 percent), and Tumblr (5 percent) less of the time.[36]

Some teens are using social media almost continuously. Most teens reported using YouTube (77 percent), TikTok (58 percent), Snapchat (51 percent), and Instagram (50 percent) every day. What's most alarming is that more than half of the teens (54 percent) say it would be difficult for them to give up using social media, and about one-third (36 percent) admit they spend too much time on social media. Girls (41 percent) were more likely than boys (31 percent) to say they spend too much time looking at social media.

Believe it or not, there's a scientific reason why teens can't put their phones down. Studies have revealed that social media activates the brain's reward center by releasing dopamine, a chemical in your brain that helps nerve cells send messages to each other. When you experience something positive, dopamine makes you feel good.

Mazzarella compares the emotional high teenagers receive from social media to consuming junk food. A Whopper and French fries might taste good, but you're probably going to feel bloated and tired a short time later. But that probably won't stop you from pulling back into the drive-thru lane a few days later. Social media is the same way.

"It starts off with an amazing flood of feel-good chemicals in one's body until you just can't quite achieve that," Mazzarella said. "It's an empty promise every time you get back online, but it's just enough to keep you sort of to the point where you just don't look around in your environment for anything else. Nothing could be as exciting as what's on a screen."

Like fast-food restaurants, teenagers keep getting back on social media apps even though it makes them feel bad sometimes. The Pew Research Center Study reported that 32 percent of the respondents believed that social media had a mostly negative effect on people their age. Interestingly, only 9 percent said social media had a negative effect on them personally.

The Pew Research Center Study also found that teens said they have positive experiences on social media because it makes them feel more connected to what's going on in their friends' lives, and it's a place where they have people who can support them through difficult times.

Other studies have revealed that teenagers and young adults are trading face-to-face interactions with their friends for FaceTime and social media. A University of Michigan study, *Monitoring the Future*, has been following young people in the United States since the 1970s. In June 2023, its national survey of high school students found that only 32 percent of seniors gathered with their friends in person nearly every day, compared to 44 percent in 2010. Social gatherings for eighth graders dropped from about two-and-a-half a week in 2000 to one-and-a-half in 2021.[37]

"That is a disturbing set of research results right there," Mazzarella said. "And it goes to show you that our resiliency is being eroded away because we don't have the sense of connection and support with our peers that we need. I mean in-person connections. Sadly, digital connections are replacing in-person connections. We need to get them out in public interacting and picking up on nonverbal cues and being able to track people with their attention, not just sit on their phones side by side and parallel play like a couple of four-year-olds."

Mazzarella believes the root of the problem starts at home. The days of families sitting down and having dinner together are mostly over. The skyrocketing prices of homes, cars, and other necessities require both parents to work, so there's no longer an authority figure at home holding down the fort and establishing routines.

"You don't have the kind of opportunities to have dinner together, for example, where you learn social skills, you learn how to listen well, you learn how to have some manners, and hopefully have a nutritious meal," Mazzarella said.

Sadly, digital connections are replacing in-person connections.

The rest of family life, in many cases, revolves around sports practices, dance routines, and other extracurricular activities.

You might be amazed at how much better putting down your phone, going outside, and reconnecting with nature will make you feel. It will improve your mood, reduce anxiety and stress, increase your physical activity, improve sleep, and boost your overall health because getting out in nature is proven to increase your immune function.

When I'm at home in Michigan, there's nothing I enjoy more than being on the water, whether it's fishing, boating, skiing, or riding a Jet Ski. When I'm at my grandparents' house in Colorado during the winter, I'm practically only inside when I'm eating dinner or sleeping. The rest of the time, I'm out discovering what one of the last great frontiers has to offer—and it's so much. I'll go cross-country skiing, downhill skiing, snowboarding, bobsledding, ice climbing, mountain biking, or hiking up some of the tallest mountains in the United States. For me, there's nothing like getting fresh air and taking advantage of what God has provided us. Given all my health problems as a kid, I kind of feel like I'm living on bonus time, and I'm going to take full advantage of it!

As I told you earlier, I love a good physical challenge. One of the most difficult runs I've completed is the Rim-to-Rim-to-Rim Trail at the Grand Canyon. It's quite a test because you first descend nine miles down a canyon wall, then across the floor for seven miles, before climbing again on one of the steepest parts of the North Kaibab Trail on the North Rim. For the last section, you must climb seven miles at a 15-percent to 20-percent grade. That's steep!

The first time I tried to run the Rim-to-Rim-to-Rim Trail in October 2022, I was recovering from a knee injury. I spent so much time favoring my good knee that it ended up killing me on the way back up. I was hobbling on two broken wheels. I completed the run again in October 2023, thankfully without much difficulty, even though I was recovering from a hamstring injury at the time.

I'm telling you: There's nothing like running through the Grand Canyon when the sun is kissing the natural wonder of the magnificent rock formations. The spectacular and ever-changing tapestry of light and shadow, from rich reds to striking oranges to brown, is unlike anything I've ever seen. Talk about a dopamine rush! I promise you can't duplicate that feeling on social media.

Another one of my most challenging adventures took me through the breathtaking Rocky Mountains. In July 2023, I competed in the Life Time Leadville Stages Races in Colorado. It's a three-day mountain bike race that covers one hundred miles. This forty-plus-year-old race takes place in Leadville, which was a booming mining town of about thirty thousand people during the Colorado Silver Boom of the late 1870s. When silver was discovered there, it became one of the richest cities in the country. After one of the largest mines closed in the 1980s, the population declined dramatically and there wasn't much industry left.

Ken Chlouber, a miner and businessman, came up with the idea to stage the Leadville Trail 100 Run, a grueling 100-mile ultramarathon, to bring tourists back to the area. He staged the first race in 1983 and it has grown into one of the most popular high-elevation endurance races in the world. Athletes from all over the world descend to Leadville every summer to compete in the "Race Across the Sky." There are a series of biking and running competitions throughout the summer.

The Leadville Stage Race, in which I competed, requires you to complete about four thousand feet of elevation each day. Competitors must complete the race in less than eleven hours to be considered an official finisher and receive a coveted belt buckle. I started training for the race at home that spring, then I went to Colorado for the month of July. I biked every day, going uphill alone in the morning and again in the evening, with my good friend Ladi Lettovsky, who climbed Kilimanjaro with me and competed in this race with me too. I have been riding bikes for a long time, but there was so much I still had to learn about navigating a mountain course, like pacing, gearing, how to angle your body when you're ascending and descending, and how to hug the frame on turns.

When race day finally arrived, I had a lot of nervous energy. I was excited but also knew it was going to be one of the most grueling tests of my life. Ladi and I gathered with 311 other competitors at Lake County Rodeo Grounds for the start of the race. The first stage would cover nearly forty miles and end at Twin Lakes Dam. Once the starter fired his gun, I was determined to ride at my own pace. My goal was to complete the first stage in well under four hours. As I started to pedal, the warm summer breeze brushed across my face. Many competitors accelerated and passed me one by one. I was unfazed and patient, knowing that the race was long, and I'd have opportunities to make up ground. I knew strategy, endurance, and discipline were going to be important. When I reached Twin Lakes Dam, I had covered 38.5 miles in about three hours and forty-one minutes. I had ascended 3,835 feet at an average speed of 10.6 mph. Not a bad start.

The next morning, my legs were sore but not too bad. I knew what was ahead of me that day: climbing Columbine, the part of the race that makes even the most experienced riders shudder. The second stage isn't as long, about twenty-two miles, but the trail is much steeper and rugged, and it takes you to the highest point of the race at 12,513 feet. Most of the course is on rock-pocked roads, so there's not much room for passing or slowing down. I'm not going to lie, once I left the sagebrush area and started the steep climb through a gorgeous aspen forest, the elevation slapped me in the face like a two-by-four.

At various points of the second stage, I had to get off my bike and carry it across rocky terrain. More experienced riders, some of them professionals, were able to navigate across the treacherous terrain. I didn't have enough experience to try. My heart rate was much higher during that part of the race, and I was having some problems breathing because of the higher elevation. When I thought I was about a quarter mile from the halfway mark, I actually wasn't anywhere close to it. I really had to dig deep to get there. I was tired. Instead of drinking water, I grabbed a Coke to try to settle my stomach down. The good news was that it was mostly all downhill from there.

It was a different challenge coming down Columbine. My heart rate was returning to normal, and I was using different muscles. My arms, hands, and legs were getting sore as I bounced my bike across rocks and ruts in the road while going about 30 mph. It was a steep descent and then back uphill again, before finally going down for good. I had been in front of Ladi for much of the day, but he came flying down the mountain and caught up with me for the last section. We ended up finishing the stage close to each other. I was proud for pushing through and completing the second stage, which had a total ascent of 3,922 feet, in about three hours and nine minutes. It was a great time and left me some wiggle room for the third stage.

Waking up on the third day, for whatever reason, I felt stronger than I did on the previous two. The final stage covered about forty-one miles from Twin Lakes Dam back to the Lake County Rodeo Grounds. It had the highest elevation gain of any of the stages at 4,872 feet. It was going to be another demanding test, especially the infamous climb up Powerline. After completing the first two stages in a combined six hours and fifty minutes, I knew I had just over four hours to finish the last one to earn a buckle. I told myself, *Let's go finish this.*

I pushed myself hard out of the gates, and Ladi and I tried to draft as close to other riders as we could. Altogether, there were probably about twenty-five of us drafting in a line once we were racing on a road. We reached another fire road and started climbing again. Even though my legs were tired from pushing through two stages of hard racing, I was determined to reach the finish line in less than eleven hours. Fortunately, I completed the final stage in about four hours and two minutes. That gave me a three-stage total of about ten hours and fifty-two minutes. I did it!

For a kid who grew up not knowing if his body would ever work like others did, completing races like the Rim-to-Rim-to-Rim Trail and Leadville Stages Races are some of my proudest achievements. But it's not only about pushing myself to the limit, it's about being one with Mother Nature and taking advantage of the incredible world that God created.

Here are some ways you can get out in nature:

- Take an outdoor fitness class.
- Hike with friends to clean up a nature trail.
- Kayak down a river.
- Take a Frisbee or football to school and throw it with a friend in the common area during lunch.
- Ask a teacher if study hall can take place outside in the sunshine.

- Instead of sitting on your bed in the darkness, do your homework on the back porch in the sun.
- Find a good book and read it on a park bench.
- Spend time in a community garden or help your parents in the yard. I'm sure they'd appreciate it!

Admittedly, I'm on social media quite a bit. Over the past couple of years, I've become active on Instagram, YouTube, Twitter, and Facebook. As an author and motivational speaker, social media gives me tremendous opportunities to reach a large audience. It's also a great way to keep up with my friends from high school and college, my relatives, and other people I want to stay in touch with. If you're following reputable media outlets, social media is also a great way to monitor the news and sports scores. In so many ways, it makes the world seem just a little bit smaller for all of us.

Take a minute to think about everything else we could be doing if we just set down our iPhones, iPads, laptops, and tablets. How much more productive would we be? How much more would we talk to each other face-to-face, instead of doing it through direct messages, tweets, and text messages? When was the last time you walked next door or across the street and had a face-to-face conversation with your neighbor?

If we decide to use Facebook, Twitter, Instagram, or TikTok, it's up to each and every one of us to attempt to make those platforms a better community. Just as you should help an elderly neighbor or someone else in need, try to bring kindness to social media as well. You probably don't realize how much power you have to change someone's day with only your fingertips.

If you and your friends work together, you can transform social media into a friendlier place. We must start somewhere. Commit to doing at least one random act of kindness on social media each day. Reach out to an old

If you and your friends work together, you can transform social media into a friendlier place.

friend. Comment politely on someone's photo. Engage in meaningful dialogue with someone, even if his or her opinion might be different than your own. Make someone smile. Or better yet, make them laugh very, very hard. Try to be *nice.*

Isn't being kind on social media so much better than making snarky or mean comments to someone you probably don't even know? Isn't it so much better to help some rise to their full potential and happiness, instead of tearing them down with criticism? Social media would be such a better place if we avoided judging and intimidating others. Truly think about what you're going to write before you send it.

Even better, pick up your phone and use it to ask a friend for real, face-to-face time. Meet up somewhere. Look them in the eyes. Hear their voices. Get some green time. Enjoy Mother Nature. Go for a run. Walk the dog. Go hiking or mountain biking. Get out on the water. Be kind. Be true to yourself.

CHAPTER TWELVE

LEARN TO FALL

As soon as I could walk, my dad put me in a pair of skis and towed me around the bunny slopes at Beaver Creek Resort in Colorado. My grandparents had built a ski-in/ski-out home there in its early development, and my parents started taking me there for holidays when I was just three months old. It became my second home.

It was by God's purpose, and not chance, that I met Ladislav Lettovsky there during the Christmas holidays in 2003. He was the good friend and mentor who climbed Mount Kilimanjaro with me. I promise we'll get back to that thrilling story at the end of the book, but, first, back up to when I was just eight years old. I had absolutely no idea how to pronounce his name. Fortunately, his nickname "Ladi" was much easier for me to remember.

My skiing skills were basic. I was easily cruising down the blue trails and could get from point A to point B on more challenging runs, but I still had a long way to go before I would be considered an advanced skier.

I had worked the previous few seasons with a different instructor, and when he informed my parents that he had a scheduling conflict, they figured he was tired of working with a kid who had bathroom challenges. They couldn't blame him.

From the moment I met Ladi I liked him immensely. Yet, I must admit that I was confused by the first skill he taught me. In my very first lesson, Ladi explained to me that we were going to practice falling. *Is he serious? That doesn't sound like much fun.* But that was exactly what we did for our first hour together. "Falling is nothing to worry about" is one of Ladi's mottos in life. He believes the only thing that prevents most people from trying new things is fear. To eliminate that fear, according to Ladi, we must first learn how to fail.

Obviously, you can't stand back up unless you fall. Think about it: We learned to fall before we walked. When we fell as babies, we didn't stop trying to walk. We learned to catch ourselves and before too long, we were running everywhere. We fall. We get back up. We learn. We grow. We live.

That first day, after learning to fall and roll, I discovered how to stand on my skis again. From that day forward, I didn't worry about falling anymore. Ladi taught me that falling wasn't as scary as I believed, and that getting back up was even more rewarding than I ever could have imagined. I've tried to apply that mantra to everything I've attempted in life.

Over the years, I learned Ladi's story during my lessons, and it became evident to me that he was never afraid of falling or trying new things. He led a life of adventure from a young age and took many chances to

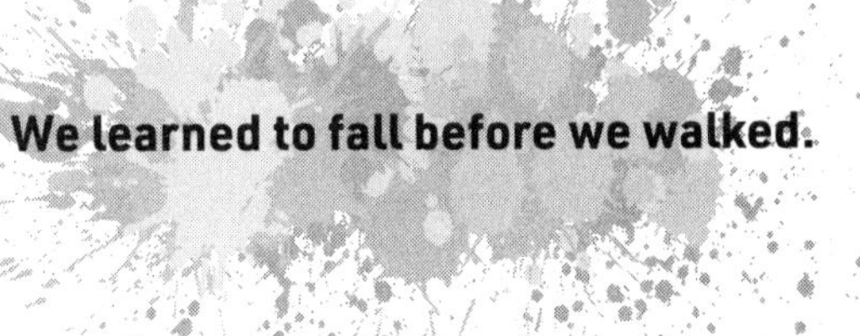

reach his full potential and obtain the life he wanted. He wasn't afraid to fall over the edge and hoped what was over the horizon was more glorious than anything he had ever seen.

Ladi grew up in the Czech city of Ostrava, located in the northeast corner of the country, about fifteen kilometers from the Polish border. When Ladi lived there in the 1960s, it was heavily industrial because of its abundance of coal. His father, also named Ladislav, had one of the most dangerous jobs in the world—working with explosives in the mines. Ladi's brother, Jindra, followed his father's footsteps and works as a mining blast technician. His mother, Vera, was a chef in a school for homeless children.

Ladi's life under communism was much simpler than what it is now in the US. Some of his fondest memories of his childhood occurred when he was part of a group that was like the Boy Scouts of America. He went to summer camp for three weeks every year, which instilled a love for nature in him. He also spent many weekends at his grandmother's house, located near a small rail station. One day, a conductor asked him if he wanted to ride on a train, which piqued his interest in transportation.

In 1976, Ladi left home at age fifteen to attend a vocational school to learn how to become a train conductor. The boarding school that Ladi attended owned a ski resort, and students operated the chair lifts as a part of their education. Ladi and his classmates stayed in a cottage near the lifts. At midnight, it was their tradition to turn the lifts on and ski at least one run, with the leader showing everyone the way by holding a cucumber jar with a lit candle since they didn't have headlamps.

Boarding school is where Ladi became an exceptional skier. When his classmates tried to teach him how to ski moguls, he struggled to keep his skis together, which is the only way you can navigate your way through large snow-covered mounds with a series of sharp turns. As a solution, his classmates locked his skis together at the bindings with a padlock and pushed him down the trail. To watch him ski moguls now, it's almost an art, as if he's dancing down the mountain.

Under Czechoslovakia's communist government, any male over sixteen years old had to serve in the military. So that he could enter the military at a higher rank, Ladi attended college first and studied computers. He then served as an air traffic controller for the Czech Air Force. He oversaw a squadron of fighter jets and planned missions. Because of the Iron Curtain's reach, his radar stretched from the Mediterranean to the Baltic Sea.

After the Soviet Union fell in 1989, Ladi's military obligation ended, and he worked as a computer programmer. Unfortunately, much of the early computer coding and programs he worked with were written in English. Someone had to translate the programs before he could use them.

Ladi married his wife, Martina, and they had their first daughter, Jane. He was determined to learn English, and he believed he could do it in about six weeks if he moved to London. He went to school and worked ten hours a day at a restaurant. His wife and daughter eventually joined him there. He received a scholarship to attend the London School of Economics, where he earned a master's degree in operations research in about a year. His studies eventually brought him to America, where he studied at the Georgia Institute of Technology in Atlanta and Cornell University in Ithaca, New York.

Eventually, Ladi relocated his family to Vail, Colorado, and he became a ski instructor at Beaver Creek Resort. During pre-season training, another instructor asked Ladi if he could help him with a double booking over the Christmas holidays. I was that client.

I ended up skiing with Ladi every winter ever since. By the time I was a teenager, he was one of my closest friends, and one of my most influential mentors. Ladi likes to say our relationship is a two-way street. While I've learned much from him about the outdoors and taking chances, Ladi says I've taught him about overcoming adversity because I've never once complained to him about my medical problems. He says I've also taught him about being grateful for everything life gives you, especially the encounters you have with other people. I'm not sure I agree with him, but Ladi says he has learned as much from me as he has taught me.

One of the attributes I respect most about Ladi is that he never stops learning. Whether it's fly-fishing, endurance racing, cooking, or hunting, Ladi is determined to try to learn new things. He's a big believer in being exposed to as many things as possible and being well rounded. He believes there's something to be learned, no matter how small, in everything you try. And, of course, he believes you learn by falling.

Another one of my good friends and mentors is Scott "Intake" Kartvedt, who is a retired US Navy fighter pilot. Scott and I met when we went skiing in Beaver Creek with a mutual friend from the Detroit area. We skied hard and were getting ready to make the final run of the day. We were tired, so we warned each other about being safe. Unfortunately, Scott clipped a tree on the way down the mountain. His patella tendon in his right leg exploded into eleven pieces. He had to be carried off the mountain. We made sure that Scott was being taken care of, went to get his wife, and packed up his luggage. He spent six weeks in a hospital bed recovering and faced months of physical therapy. Less than a year later, he was back on the slopes. If you knew anything about Scott's story, you wouldn't be surprised.

Scott grew up in San Diego, California. His mother attempted suicide twice while he was a kid. His father had financial problems, bankrupted his law firm, and lost the family's home. Eventually, Scott's parents divorced.

Scott's life changed in high school when he and his buddies went to the movie theater to see *Top Gun*. Scott was so enthralled by the action that he went back to watch the movie again and again. He wore a leather jacket and aviator sunglasses. Scott and his buddies spent many afternoons at the Naval Air Station in Miramar, California, watching F-14 fighter jets take off and land.

"The air literally shook, and the roar of their engines rumbled through our chests like thunder," Scott wrote in his book, *Full Throttle: From the Blue Angels to Hollywood Stunt Pilot*. "Closer, the smell of jet fuel would have been thick, almost suffocating. The smell coated our tongues and almost numbed them. The air around the jets crackled and popped like a campfire, and as they accelerated and took off, the heat washed over us like a wave."[38]

There's no question about it: Scott was hooked on the need for speed and flying. His grandfather had served in the navy in World War II, and his dad attended the United States Naval Academy. Scott took a detour to Pepperdine University in Malibu, California, where he graduated with a degree in accounting. He was working at an accounting firm after college in the fall of 1989 when his best friend, Bobby Brust, called and told him he was joining the Air Force. Flying fighter jets had been Scott's dream, so he told his friend, "Well, then I'm going to do it too."

Scott picked up a phone book and searched for the number to a navy recruiting office in Los Angeles. When Scott told a recruiter that he wanted to fly jets off aircraft carriers, the man told him, "So does everybody."

"Yeah, but I think I can do it," Scott said.

Scott filled out an application and took all the required physical examinations and aptitude tests. He didn't hear back from the navy for more than a year. When Scott was finally accepted into aviation training, the US was involved in an aerial bombing campaign against Iraq known as Operation Desert Storm. He went to Aviation Officer Candidate School in Pensacola, Florida, and graduated in November 1991. He graduated number two in his class during flight school and got to choose his next destination: F/A-18 Hornets training in Jacksonville, Florida.

By the time Scott's twenty-one-year career in active duty in the navy ended, he had served three tours in Iraq and two in Afghanistan. He had flown more than ninety combat missions and logged over five hundred combat hours. He was awarded the Bronze Star for heroic service in a combat zone and helped establish the navy's first stealth fighter squadron.

Even more impressive, Scott flew with the US Navy Blue Angels, the world-famous flight demonstration squadron that performs thrilling aerobatic maneuvers and high-speed, close formation flying at air shows and other events around the country. He is now president of the Blue Angels Foundation and works to prevent suicides by former service members.

Scott still works as a commercial pilot and flight instructor for United Airlines. His life came full-circle the past couple of years when he worked as a stunt pilot for Tom Cruise in the 2023 blockbuster film *Top Gun: Maverick*. That's right: Scott flew the fight scenes for the pilot who had inspired him to jump into a cockpit as a teenager. Scott spent two weeks preparing for an eight-minute scene in the movie. If you've seen the film, it's the moment when Maverick and Goose's son, Rooster, steal an enemy Tomcat and fight an enemy jet to escape. It's the most exciting scene in the movie, if you ask me. Scott also worked with Cruise in another movie, *Mission: Impossible–Dead Reckoning: Part Two*, which will be released in 2025.

There's no question that Scott's life has been extraordinary and inspiring. Like Ladi, I know he has had a profound impact on me. Scott has lived his life on the foundation of three tenets: Say yes to opportunities and refuse to accept no, learn from mistakes, and ask others for help.

The perfect illustration of those principles occurred during Scott's third year flying for the Blue Angels. He

Say yes to opportunities and refuse to accept no, learn from mistakes, and ask others for help.

learned that NASA was accepting applications for astronauts. Scott had always wanted to fly to space, so he decided he was going to apply. When he told his Blue Angels peers about his idea, they joked that he would never be accepted.

"Hey, Intake, you're never going to be an astronaut," they told him. "You're not an engineer. You didn't go to test pilot school. You were an accountant. The only way you're going to space is in a cage so they can study you."[39]

Scott brushed off their jokes with a good attitude. Even though the application process would take much time by getting recommendations, undergoing physicals, and studying for aptitude tests, he thought the rewards were greater than the risks. The only thing that applying was going to cost him was his time. Becoming an astronaut and flying to space would be more than worth the effort.

"Look, I'm already not an astronaut," Scott told his friends. "So, they could come back and say, 'We don't accept your application. You're not an astronaut.' Well, I'm already not an astronaut. All it did was cost my time. But they might come back and say, 'Congratulations, we want you to come in and try to be an astronaut, right? You're going to get an interview.'"

Unfortunately, NASA didn't accept Scott's application. But the experience and excitement he felt about possibly having a chance to fly to space was well worth it. He knew NASA was never going to pick up the phone out of the blue and call him.

"I had to step forward and try," Scott said. "When I'm sixty, people might say, 'Oh, I could have been an astronaut. I wish I would've been a fighter pilot. I should have been a Blue Angel.' I can tell them, 'Yeah, I tried all those things and some of them I succeeded, and some of them I didn't. But you know what? I tried to do all of it.'"

These days, Scott speaks to students at high schools around the country every year and encourages them to take chances and never squander opportunities.

"I faced the same challenges that many young kids face with broken homes, financial challenges, parents that live paycheck to paycheck, not being able to have the things that they want or that they think will make them cool or accepted," Scott said. "Those things don't matter as much as the integrity, the character, and the principles that guide your life. So, I reach back to my life story to let them know that I am no different."

I'd encourage you to find mentors like Ladi and Scott. It's amazing what you can learn from them. Luke Skywalker wouldn't have defeated Darth Vader without the guidance of Obi-Wan Kenobi and Yoda in *Star Wars*. Frodo would have never destroyed the One Ring without Gandalf's wisdom in *The Lord of the Rings*. Katniss would have never survived *The Hunger Games* without the help of Haymitch Abernathy. Learning from those who have already experienced what you want to learn is paramount in your development.

What have you been afraid to try? What's holding you back from your next adventure? Failure is simply a stepping-stone on your way to success. Of course, this doesn't mean that it's easy to deal with or something that should be taken lightly, but how you deal with failure will determine not only your future success, but also how easy it will be to achieve. Everyone has different coping mechanisms and ways they react to failure. However, learning the ways that more often lead you to success can help you enormously!

Here are some tips on how to pick yourself up after you fall:

1. **Learn from your failure.** There is a lesson to be learned each time you fall. Discover what this lesson is and keep it in mind during future attempts at success. If you don't learn from your difficult times, you'll keep repeating the same mistakes.
2. **Forge ahead.** It's completely normal to feel like giving up when you're first hit by roadblocks. The most important part of your challenge is what you do afterwards. So, strive to have confidence in yourself. This experience may very well be your last step before you reach great success!
3. **Surround yourself with good people.** It's a good idea to be surrounded by like-minded and positive people. This is especially important when you're dealing with the negative emotions that may accompany falling down. Positive people like Ladi will inspire you to pick yourself up and go further than you thought you could go.
4. **Set goals.** If you've come up short at a large task, think about setting smaller, immediate goals. If you build your way up to completing a difficult task using small steps, each step may not feel so overwhelming. When you're finished, you'll be amazed at what you achieved!

5. **Visualize your dreams.** Fight the negative thoughts that creep up after falling short by visualizing yourself meeting your goal. Take the time to picture yourself successfully going through each step it will take to reach your goal.
6. **Be enthusiastic.** When you first set out to achieve something big, chances are you approached the task at hand with a great deal of enthusiasm. If you meet challenges once or even several times, it's important to maintain the enthusiastic force to give you the energy and drive to continue toward your goal.
7. **Write it down.** Keep a journal that details your personal thoughts, goals, and attempts. It will help you stay organized and focused on success. Another good exercise is to write your goal on a piece of paper and place it somewhere where you can see it several times each day to remind yourself to act toward this desire.
8. **Don't dwell in the past.** The past doesn't have to be your present or future. Just because you had a setback, it doesn't mean that it will continue to be the case. The only way to achieve your goals is to keep trying.
9. **Think about the worst-case scenario.** What's the worst thing that can happen if you have a hard time achieving goals? Some people are so concerned with success and have such a horrible

> fear of failure that they don't consider whether the worst-case scenario is all that bad! Realizing that obstacles may only mean a small delay toward your eventual success can alleviate some of your fears and give you the confidence to succeed. Just keep plowing ahead and remember that there are no bad days—only hard ones!

Just keep trying. It's likely that you can think of someone you know who set his or her mind on a goal

The most important thing I've learned is that God will get you back on your feet.

and would stop at nothing to achieve it. It's not just some kind of story or fantasy—this could be *you* too! Adopt this drive and apply it to your situation. When you believe in yourself and your abilities, you'll gain the drive to keep moving forward and you'll feel unstoppable.

The most important thing I've learned is that God will get you back on your feet. Don't be afraid to fail. Fall apart. Put yourself back together. Fall behind. Get back in front. Fall down. Get back up. Fall off. Get back on. Don't stop falling or trying. There's nothing more rewarding than putting yourself back together. Trust me, after everything I've endured in my life, I would know.

CHAPTER THIRTEEN

FIND YOUR WOLF PACK

ONE OF MY FAVORITE MOVIES IS *THE HANGOVER*, which follows the unforgettable exploits of a small bachelor party in Las Vegas. In one of the opening scenes, Alan Garner, the eccentric brother of the bride who is played by the hilarious actor Zach Galifianakis, makes an uncomfortable speech on the roof of Caesars Palace. He talks about how he was a bit of a loner until his sister brought home her soon-to-be husband, Doug.

"I tend to think of myself as a one-man wolf pack," Alan tells the group. "But when my sister brought Doug home, I knew he was one of my own. And my wolf pack, it grew by one. So there . . . there were two of us in the wolf pack."[40]

After Doug invited Alan to his bachelor party and introduced him to his good friends, Stu Price and Phil Wenneck, his wolf pack became even bigger.

"And six months ago, when Doug introduced me to you guys, I thought, 'Wait a second, could it be?'" Alan continued. "And now I know for sure, I just added two more guys to my wolf pack. Four of us wolves, running around the desert together, in Las Vegas."

Finding your wolf pack, or tribe, is essential in your growth as a person. Surrounding yourself with people who can help you grow, both spiritually and personally, is integral to your well-being. It's so important to find

your tribe, whether it's family, friends, co-workers, or people who might have the same interests and hobbies as you. We can't do life alone. Surround yourself with people who inspire you and lift you up. Build meaningful relationships in which you and your friends will have deeper connections. Those are the kind of bonds that last a lifetime.

It's important to surround yourself with people who share the same values. Don't sacrifice your integrity and reputation to make friends or be part of the "cool" group. Find people who will have a positive influence on you, those who are interested in helping you grow as a person. If you don't, you might wake up in a hotel room in Las Vegas with a tiger in the bathroom like Alan and his wolf pack!

Loyalty is the basis of any meaningful relationship, and wolves are the perfect illustration. Within the pack, unity and working together is not just a choice but also a necessity. If the wolves don't act as one, they'll starve, be eaten by predators, or become extinct. They share a responsibility for protecting each other and put their lives on the line to ensure their loved ones are safe. Wolves put their personal aspirations aside for the greater good of the pack. True friends are the same way. They'll remain loyal through thick and thin. They won't lead you down the wrong path to danger.

In August 2014, I made the bold move to leave my nest when I left the comfortable surroundings of my parents' home for High Point University in North Carolina. For the first time in my life, I was going to be alone to stand up for myself and fight for the accommodations I would need to be a successful college student.

Of course, there were still going to be plenty of people there to support me. At High Point, every freshman is assigned to a life coach, and mine was a wonderful man named Akir Khan, who had worked in the George W. Bush administration as a liaison to the

Muslim community before joining High Point, where he was working toward a doctorate in educational leadership.

In our first meeting, Dr. Khan told me, "I want you to know I'll always have your back, JT. I've experienced similar things. For example, I had bad enough asthma that I couldn't be in sports or join the military like I wanted to. I never let it stop me, but it was hard. That's why I'm thrilled today to be a mentor to students and help them develop their game plans."

Remember what I wrote about having a great mentor? I had found another one. I met with Dr. Khan once a week and eventually he told me that I had a "growth mindset," which is an ability to adapt to difficult situations and a willingness to be uncomfortable so that I could learn outside the box and evolve. If he only knew how I was used to being uncomfortable!

As I told you earlier, Mom and Dad were my biggest advocates when I was younger, but I assumed the role for myself in high school and would need to do so even more in college. Eventually, my parents taught me to stand on my own. They told me to take ownership of my struggles and problems and learn how to solve them. They gave me additional responsibilities as I grew older, and they talked through potential solutions when I couldn't figure things out. At High Point, it was up to me, not my parents, to ask for accommodations because of my learning differences, and the university and its faculty and staff weren't going to offer them without me first asking.

Colleges don't fall under the Individuals with Disabilities Education Act, which is why there are no IEPs like there are in high school. But most colleges have a disability services office for students with learning and thinking differences, and I worked with employees in that office to come up with a plan on how I could succeed at High Point. At the beginning

They told me to take ownership of my struggles and problems and learn how to solve them.

of my first semester as a freshman, my accommodations letter stated that I could record the lectures in class. I could also request copies of lecture notes. I was permitted to use alternative versions of textbooks, such as audio recordings, which I used while I read. For exams, I was able to take the tests in a distraction-reduced room, could use software that read the exam to me and recorded my oral responses, and I was afforded more time to complete the work.

I will admit that these accommodations were the difference in me passing or failing every course that I took during my four years at High Point. Some of the faculty went out of their way to help me complete my work despite my short-term memory and reading issues, and I will forever be grateful and thankful for their dedication, empathy, and kindness.

For example, the professor in my first history course, American Aspirations, came to understand that I had difficulties getting my answers and ideas down on paper. So, the professor, Dr. Kara Dixon Vuic, decided for me to come to class early when we were having a test or quiz, then stayed with me afterward to go through my answers orally to make sure I was getting my point across.

However, some of my professors wouldn't budge when it came to certain rules, although they were kind to me when they explained their reasoning. For instance, High Point didn't allow anyone to use calculators on math tests—period. Without a calculator, I bombed my first big math test. I conferred with my Learning Excellence academic coach, Heather Slocum, who helped me request to use a calculator in a revised accommodations letter. When I approached the math professor with the letter, however, she still wouldn't change her mind.

Through these trials and struggles, I earned a deeper awareness of what I can and cannot do well and how to compensate for my shortcomings. At times, it was extremely stressful, but I ultimately learned a valuable lesson. I was out of the nest and comforts of my home for the first time, but I was determined to advocate for myself.

Fortunately, I had a wide support system in place. Julie Martin Kelly, my tutor from home, was still working with me. She had copies of my textbooks and assignments and helped me break down the material and concentrate on what I needed to know. She also helped me tremendously with time management and learning how to study properly and efficiently. We met via Skype four times each week, and working with her provided me with the confidence I needed to pass my classes and juggle everything on my plate.

The Learning Excellence office, including Suzanne Hawks, Dr. Craig Curty, and Pamala Wannamaker, helped me keep my head up when I struggled with a lesson or didn't do well on a test. Mrs. Slocum helped me create weekly to-do lists and calendars, and she reviewed material with me.

Even though I received help from many different people who truly cared about me and very much wanted me to succeed, I also came to realize that I had to learn the material, understand it, and do the work on my own. Ultimately, it was up to me to put in the necessary time and effort to pass my classes, regardless of whatever accommodations and assistance I was receiving.

At the time, I was reminded of a column that my mother had shared with me a few years earlier. Kendra

Graham, the wife of the evangelist Will Graham, was the author. Doctors had diagnosed one of their three daughters with dyslexia in the second grade. She compared her daughter's learning disability to the formation of a pearl:

> [A] pearl is formed in an oyster because of an irritation that finds its way to the inside of the shell. The oyster wraps the irritation with a coat of mother of pearl. The larger the irritation, the more coats of this substance are used to wrap around the point of pain until, in the end, the irritation is gone, but a beautiful costly pearl is formed. Often the things for which we have to work hardest are the things we treasure the most.[41]

Graham wrote that her daughter had to work harder than her sisters. Assignments that should have taken ten minutes took an hour or more to complete. Like me, her daughter has to learn something and then learn it again and again until it gets stuck in her brain. She watched her daughter get mad and frustrated, and then she wondered, *Why her? Why not me?*

One day, as Graham and her daughter worked through an assignment that was taking much longer than it should have, she decided to simply complete the work for her. Her daughter glanced up and said, "Don't steal my pearl! It's my treasure!"

"Letting our children struggle is hard, but God has entrusted this testimony to my daughter. I can stand beside her and support her, but the battle is hers—as is the treasure,"[42] she wrote.

After all my trials and tribulations, after all my hard work and the help from so many others who loved me, raised me up along the way, and encouraged me to do my best, my pearl came in the form of a bachelor of science in business administration degree from High Point University. I graduated with a GPA of 3.21.

Of course, my mother and father were there to see me get my diploma, along with both sets of my grandparents, when I walked across the stage at the Promenade in the center of the High Point campus on May 5, 2018. The singer-actor-philanthropist Josh Groban delivered the commencement speech, the first of his life, on that very muggy day. His speech truly pulled at my heart that day; he talked about change, taking chances, and risks.

I know one thing: I couldn't have experienced what I did at High Point and taken so many risks without the wonderful tribe surrounding me. Who would be in your tribe or wolf pack? Write down the names of three people you might want to be friends with. Reflect on their strengths and weaknesses. Do they have the same characteristics you want people to recognize in you? If not, find someone else to be in your tribe. The pursuit of your tribe never ends. I know that was certainly the case for me, as we searched for teachers, tutors, specialists, and doctors who could help me learn to read and write.

If your parents, grandparents, or teachers are like mine, you've probably heard the phrase, "You are who your friends are," more than once in your life. There's so much truth to that statement. It's important to regularly assess the company we keep. You should surround yourself with people who will serve as a positive influence for you, and you should try to uplift your friends and peers

It's important to regularly assess the company we keep.

as well. While we can all strive to be the moral compass of a group, we can be more influential by being part of a morally sound collective that can make an impact on an entire class, school, or community.

Today, the people who influence us, both positively and negatively, extend beyond the personal interactions we have at school, work, or social settings. The people we follow on social media platforms as well as those we see on TV and listen to on Spotify and podcasts, significantly shape our character too. It's important to weigh and evaluate the digital connections you're making as well.

While *The Hangover* is a comedy and many of the scenes were exaggerated to be hilariously funny, the plot does highlight how our friends' actions and decisions can affect our lives. Alan, Doug, Stu, and Phil found themselves in more than a few precarious situations because of Alan's poor choices at the beginning of the night. The aftermath underscores the importance of surrounding yourself with reliable and responsible friends and building your wolf pack with good, solid people. If you don't, you might find yourself being on the wrong end of Mike Tyson's left hook, and that is certainly no fun!

CHAPTER FOURTEEN

LEAVE A LEGACY

If you grew up in Detroit, the Motor City, you probably have a deep love of automobiles. My dad and I love cars, especially fast ones, and especially the ones made right here in Detroit with American blood, sweat, and tears.

Unless you grew up in the 1940s and 1950s like my grandparents did, you might not know that Detroit is famous for something else. After the United States agreed to join the Allies to defeat Nazi Germany and the Axis powers in World War II, the Motor City became the center of America's military production. Instead of building Fords, Chryslers, and Chevrolets, Detroit's auto factory workers produced tanks, munitions, airplanes, radar units, Jeeps, amphibious vehicles, and bullets.

My late grandfather, John Boll, was the son of Dutch immigrants. His mother and father came to the

US shortly after they married, and they didn't know a word of English. They settled in Detroit, where my grandfather was born in 1929. After high school, Papi, as I called him, joined the US Army in 1951, six years after the Allies had defeated the Nazis. He met my grandmother, Marlene, when he was stationed at Fort Bragg, North Carolina. She was a dancer with the Roxy Theatre Chorus Line, or the Roxyettes, who performed at a theatre located just off Times Square in New York. They were performing at the North Carolina state fair and had missed their ride to the fairgrounds. Papi and a couple of his buddies picked them up, and the ladies gave them tickets to their show to thank them. The rest, as they say, is history. They were married on June 19, 1954, and moved back to Detroit.

Papi started a construction company–literally with a wheelbarrow and shovel in his car's trunk–and completed odd jobs around town. A couple of years later, he partnered with someone to start an excavating business. In 1964, Papi founded Chateau Estates, a developer of manufactured home communities. Eventually, his properties were home to twenty thousand families throughout Michigan and Florida.

To give back to the Detroit community, Nani and Papi established the John A. and Marlene L. Boll Foundation in 1985. Over the last thirty-eight years, the foundation has pledged more than $50 million in support of the arts, education, and health services in

Michigan, around the US, and across the world. My grandparents are grateful for the way God has blessed our family, and they want to be faithful stewards of the resources entrusted in their care. Papi passed away on August 24, 2022. He was ninety-three years old. He will always be one of my heroes.

What will your legacy be? How will others remember you and your life after you are gone? Our legacies are passed from one generation to the next, and in many

What will your legacy be? How will others remember you and your life after you are gone?

cases it's the only thing we leave behind. How we live our lives and the actions we take each day are how people will remember us. Whether at work, school, church, or home, how we treat others and how we act around them will shape our legacies.

It's like the American statesman Benjamin Franklin wrote, "If you would not be forgotten as soon as you are dead, either write something worth reading or do something worth writing."[43] Or as the legendary poet Maya

Angelou once said, "If you're going to live, leave a legacy. Make a mark on the world that can't be erased."[44]

There are plenty of young people doing exactly that. You might have seen the film *Soul Surfer*, which documents the incredible story of Bethany Hamilton. Bethany grew up in Hawaii. Both of her parents were avid surfers, and they exposed her to the islands' massive waves when she was young. Bethany dreamed of becoming a professional surfer and secured her first sponsorship when she was nine.

On October 31, 2003, Bethany and her good friend, Alana Blanchard, were surfing at Tunnels Beach on the north shore of Kauai. Bethany was lying on her surfboard stomach-down with her left arm dangling in the water. As Bethany was talking to Alana and Alana's father and brother, the unimaginable happened: A fourteen-foot tiger shark attacked her. The shark bit off her left arm below the shoulder. The Blanchards helped Bethany paddle back to shore, and Alana's father fashioned a tourniquet around her arm. By the time Bethany reached a hospital, she was in shock and had lost about 60 percent of her blood. She underwent several surgeries and survived.

Incredibly, only three weeks later, Bethany returned to the water and was surfing again. After adjusting her technique to compensate for the loss of her left arm, Bethany was surfing in competitions within a year and won her first national title in 2005. At the age of seventeen, she realized her dream by competing in the World Surf League.

Bethany wrote the book *Soul Surfer: A True Story of Faith, Family, and Fighting to Get Back on the Board*, and in 2011 the *Soul Surfer* film was released. Bethany has written additional books to inspire others who are facing seemingly insurmountable setbacks in their lives. Her Beautifully Flawed Foundation helps young people who are living with limb differences and those who have experienced traumatic limb loss. As the foundation's website says, "The name 'Beautifully Flawed' came from the concept that no matter what 'flaws' we may have, God loves us and sees us as beautiful. He can use the pain and the trials we face in life for a greater purpose."[45]

"The world's not perfect; you're going to face pain or struggles or things that are going to bring you down," Hamilton told *HAWAI'I Magazine*. "You're going to have to choose and make choices that will either bring you down or up. We just have to be kind of ready for whatever comes our way, no matter what it ends up being."[46]

Bethany is changing lives around the world as a motivational speaker and through her foundation. She hosts retreats for young women and men who have experienced limb loss and conferences to help young girls and women "discover their true beauty, purpose, and worth." The foundation's first response team sends care packages to shark attack victims. Her foundation helped victims of the Boston Marathon bombing. She went to

Thailand shortly after a tsunami devastated the country and worked with children to help them overcome their fear of the ocean.

"As I grew up with one arm and relearned how to surf, God taught me that He can take the hard times that I went through and turn them into something beautiful," Bethany said during a convocation at Liberty University. "I think that He can do that for each and every one of you. He can take what you have been through and use it for good if you are willing to share what He has done for you."[47]

Lily, a resilient nursing student at a private college out West, is another young woman who has overcome numerous challenges in her remarkable journey. Born in China with a tethered spinal cord and other serious medical conditions, Lily faced early challenges, moving from her biological mother's care to an orphanage and foster home. Her parents became her unwavering support system, adopting her when she was five years old. The first time Lily met them, she could only take a few steps before falling because she didn't have much strength in her right leg.

Soon after Lily moved to the US, her parents took her to a children's hospital in Cincinnati, Ohio. Doctors discovered that she had VACTERL syndrome, including a barely functioning kidney, clubfoot, a spine that wasn't fully developed, and many of the same plumbing issues that I have. She had a procedure to correct her tethered spinal cord and then pelvic surgery about a year later. A Malone procedure to improve her plumbing soon followed.

Along with her parents, her brothers and younger sister are her biggest advocates. Her parents also adopted Maggie from China. Despite facing many medical challenges, Lily excelled in school. She was salutatorian of her senior class in high school. She was accepted into the nursing program at her college; she decided to major in that area because she had met so many fantastic nurses throughout her medical journey.

"The nurses that I had were just amazing, and they really did impact me during those days in the hospital," Lily said. "It just solidified my desire to pursue nursing. That's what I also want to do: to be able to communicate with families and help them troubleshoot the everyday issues that they may face."[48]

While Lily's friends in high school and college have been empathetic about her medical condition, she found solace at Youth Rally, a one-of-a-kind camp that brings together young people with bowel and bladder differences from all around the country. The first time Lily attended Youth Rally in Seattle, Washington, when she was thirteen, she discovered she wasn't too different and wasn't alone in her journey.

"That camp really did change my life," Lily said. "My mom was like, 'Yeah, from the day that I dropped you off and the day that I picked you up, you were different.'

Something about you changed and you suddenly had more confidence and were more expressive."

Youth Rally had such a profound effect on Lily's life and self-esteem that she now works at the camp as a counselor.

"You really get to see in real time how, as the week goes by, how much kids come out of their shell and are able to just be goofy, make poop jokes, and talk about their stuff openly with everyone there," Lily said. "Now,

Live the way you want others to remember you.

obviously that doesn't always translate into what we call the real world because Youth Rally's sort of like a little oasis-type place where you can talk about anything and nothing is ever taboo. But over the years, you can just see the kids growing more confident, and each year they come back with more livelihood."

Every time Lily and her friends go back to Youth Rally, they call it a family reunion. Helping younger kids with medical challenges, as a camp counselor and nurse, will be part of her legacy. Her story is a testament to her resilience, determination, and unwavering commitment to making a positive impact in the lives of others.

What will your legacy be? Fortunately, there is still time to build it. If you don't have the financial resources to be charitable, give your time, God-given talents, and emotional support to those in need. Think about how you treat others at work or school. Smile and greet your fellow students or employees, offer them compliments, and encourage them whenever you can. Mentor younger employees at work, or, if you're an older student in school, take a freshman or sophomore under your wings, show them the ropes, and look out for them. Most importantly, act like someone others will want to look up to—be nice! Live the way you want others to remember you.

And, of course, always be kind.

When you have faced as many health obstacles as I have, you think about your life and legacy often. Hopefully, I've made a positive impact on my family, friends, schools, and communities with my faith, attitude, empathy, and spirit. I sure hope I have had a positive effect on the people I love. I know I have worked hard to be that kind of person.

Just a couple of years ago, I decided to follow in my grandparents' footsteps and establish the JT Mestdagh Foundation. My hope is that by "reaching up and reaching out, the JT Mestdagh Foundation sees a world changed and improved by children with congenital colorectal issues who receive world-class medical care, and by those with dyslexia and other learning differences who excel with the best possible educational testing, mentoring, and tutoring, especially using the Tattum Reading program." My foundation also "envisions these young people's families, caregivers, and educators surrounded with love and hope as well as practical tools and creative strategies to ease the demands that no one should face alone."

When I was growing up, my parents and I faced those same obstacles and challenges alone because the proper testing, mentoring, and tutoring weren't in place. I didn't know how to read–and feared that I would never learn how–until God intervened. I was blessed to meet Steve Tattum, who changed my life forever. My parents and I remain steadfastly committed to bringing the Tattum F.A.S.T. reading program to the Grosse Pointe Public School System, as well as other school districts around Michigan to help students with learning differences.

I'm also excited that Steve is working with Beyond Basics, a student and family-centered, literacy-focused nonprofit organization in Detroit. Beyond Basics has been around since 1999, and its president, Pamela Good, started working with Steve three years later to better serve its students. Beyond Basics says it consistently helps students achieve grade level reading in six to ten weeks with one-on-one tutoring programs and Steve's programs. In 2018, Detroit Public Schools had the lowest standardized test scores in the country with 95 percent of fourth graders not being proficient in reading and 93 percent not being proficient in math. There are so many students there who need our help.

Today, Beyond Basics has more than 1,500 volunteers and forty-seven staff members who are helping thousands of students in metropolitan Detroit schools learn to read and write. In October 2018, with the help of General Motors, Beyond Basics opened the doors to the Beyond Basics Family Literacy Center, which helps

I'm working hard every day to be remembered as they one day will be.

teach families to read and provides help with GED and SAT preparation, essay writing support, and workplace development programs. Pamela and her staff are doing such great work.

Hopefully, with my work in helping children and adults learn to read and write, and the work I'm doing to help children with VATER syndrome and other congenital colorectal issues, I'll leave a legacy that my children and grandchildren will one day be proud of. I know one thing for certain: I couldn't be prouder of my grandparents. I'm working hard every day to be remembered as they one day will be. I'm trying to be kind, considerate, and generous.

I know one thing: I'm going to keep a smile on my face and try to make the people around me happy.

CHAPTER FIFTEEN

KEEP CLIMBING

On the crisp morning of October 7, 2018, we bid farewell to Barranco Camp on Mount Kilimanjaro, perched at an elevation of about 13,020 feet above sea level. Fully aware that the daunting summit, Uhuru Peak, was still a long way off, I prayed to God to give me the strength and wisdom to complete the challenge and keep us safe.

Our journey began amid breathtaking scenery, following the path along a river with cascading waterfalls. When we rose from moorland terrain, we transitioned into the arid expanse of the brown alpine desert. While many climbers head south through the Karanga Valley to merge with the Mweka Route for a southern approach to Uhuru Peak, our expedition would follow a more distinct and danger route. We were embarking on a seldom-used northern route, passing by Lava Tower Camp and then north to Arrow Glacier, before ultimately tackling the treacherous Western Breach.

As the altitude increased, so did the chill in the air. When we reached a targeted ridge, I took a moment to glance at the altimeter hooked to the shoulder strap of my daypack. The digital display read 14,439 feet—the exact altitude of the highest peak I'd been on at Mt. Elbert! I

I prayed to God to give me the strength and wisdom to complete the challenge and keep us safe.

took a moment to reflect on this personal achievement, but I knew in my heart that there was a much taller peak that I still wanted to tackle.

We continued to follow our guide Simon's rhythmic lead of *pole, pole*. However, as we got closer to our destination, Arrow Glacier Camp, nestled at the foot of the foreboding Western Breach, I wasn't feeling too well. The pressure in my head was a warning sign of what might soon be coming. I prepared myself for the inevitability that I would probably suffer altitude sickness the next day. I knew I'd have to stay hydrated, fueled up, and keep plenty of Advil in my pocket.

That night, our skilled cook, Christopher Agga, made us a wonderful dinner, and my good friend and mentor Ladi handed me a helmet—a stark reminder of the danger that was awaiting us on the Western Breach.

That night, I went to sleep earlier because we were starting extremely early the next day, around 4:00 a.m. It was the day I had dreamed about for so long—the day I hoped to conquer Mount Kilimanjaro's peak! Despite the unease in my stomach and head, I was determined to finish my journey and join the rare fraternity of climbers who reached Uhuru Peak.

The Western Breach is so dangerous that Simon won't guide climbers up that route anymore—at least that's what his company's website says. Yet, in typical Ladi fashion, persuasion prevailed. The Western Breach, as its name suggests, is a gap on the western outer rim of Kili's main summit, Kibo. Lava flow formed it hundreds of years ago, which caused a massive collapse of part of the summit. Thick layers of ice, albeit diminished over time, coat the high rim, binding geologic debris into place.

When I woke up at 4:00 a.m. the next day, even the ice covering the inside of my tent couldn't dampen my excitement. My headache was gone, and I felt invigorated and well rested. Simon's assistant guide, Manase, took my vitals, and my oxygen level was sufficient. I had a hearty breakfast of oatmeal and raisins, full of iron, which was good for my blood at altitudes that high. Mindful of plummeting temperatures near the summit, we filled our water bottles with a mixture of cold and hot water so they wouldn't freeze. I strapped on my helmet and headlamp and was ready to finish the mission.

In the predawn darkness, Simon went over our planned route with us one more time. A handful of the porters descended for supplies. The remaining ones stayed with us and carried critical emergency oxygen and medical equipment. With Arrow Glacier Camp fading behind us, we started the final ascent at 5:26 a.m., charting a course east-southwardly—and straight up.

Back home, my parents were nervously following our progress on my website. My Garmin GPS posted a little dot every thirty minutes to show them where we were on a digital topography map. Slowly, they watched as we reached 16,029 feet, 16,518 feet, 16,885 feet and so on.

We had to be exceptionally careful crossing the steep snowfields in the dark. *Pole, pole* echoed with even greater importance. One false step could send one of us sliding down a perilous fall thousands of feet below. We used our ice picks and hiking poles to make each step. Crossing the Western Breach in the dark might seem crazy, but falling rocks were less likely in sub-freezing temperatures. It was paramount that we cross the danger zone before daybreak, so here we were following Simon with only the light from our headlamps.

After a couple of hours of careful climbing, we crossed the Western Breach and paused at a collection of boulders to catch our breath. Here, Simon, with a solemn tone, delivered a stark warning: "My friends, we are at the point of no turning back."

Simon said it would be too difficult to climb back down once we started our ascent on the Rock Steps, our next challenge. Even if one of us was badly injured, the

We were at the footsteps of our goal, the summit within reach.

only way down was to press on, climbing an additional five hundred feet into a crater and then crossing it for a mile to begin our descent to the nearest camp.

I exchanged glances with Ladi, who then looked at Martina. They both turned and glanced at me. The collective smiles on our faces spoke volumes—there was no way we were turning back now. We were at the footsteps of our goal, the summit within reach.

However, only fifteen minutes later, doubt cast its shadow. Immediately above us was a false summit.

From a distance, it looked like the top of Kili. Once we reached the deceptive peak, there was another ridge with more terrain beyond it. Undeterred, we kept climbing.

Soon after, my stomach started to cramp with hot pain. It felt like it was boiling. A wave of nausea hit me. I was in pain but pushed on, without telling Ladi and Martina. I knew I had to get to a toilet—as soon as possible!

My upset stomach was the result of a bug, which I believed I'd probably contracted from drinking untreated water. Because of my compromised intestinal system, I also was starting to feel signs of altitude sickness. The summit was two hours away. Would I get so sick that Simon and Manase would have to carry me to the top? Worse, in my mind, would Ladi and Martina sacrifice their dream of getting there because of me? Fortunately for me, Martina is a registered nurse and knew what to do immediately. She worked to keep me hydrated and started me on antibiotics.

In the blinding sunlight, we finally crawled over the rocky Western Breach rim into Kibo's caldera. A stunning white mile-wide expanse greeted us. We started climbing a rock field up many ridges toward Kibo's Furtwängler Glacier, what was left of the ice cap that once covered all of Kilimanjaro.

We still had an hour to go, and we were getting tired. Fighting my exhaustion, I pushed on behind Simon, with Manase and the medical porter in the rear. When I felt nausea taking over, I found a boulder and threw up for the first time. Unfortunately, it wouldn't be the last. I began to realize I was getting weak. Ladi tried to calm me by walking with me at a *pole, pole* pace.

I was thirty minutes from the top of Mount Kilimanjaro—and from accomplishing one of my lifelong dreams—and I wasn't stopping now. Head down, I forged onward and upward, ignoring my mounting fatigue and discomfort in my stomach.

Suddenly, the slope leveled out and there, in the not-so-far distance, a mere fifty feet away, I saw it. It was the wooden, hand-painted sign that marks Kili's summit—a global sign of triumph. Adrenaline surged through me, and I started running with Martina. Ladi, seizing the moment, grabbed the camera and started videotaping us.

At precisely 11:28 a.m. on October 7, 2018, after climbing more than 3,300 feet in about seven hours, we stood at the summit of Mount Kilimanjaro. I thanked Martina and hugged her. I hugged Ladi. I hugged Simon. I hugged Manase. Just being up there with them made me think about how amazing our God is. After battling so many medical problems as a child and teenager, I often wondered whether I would be able to do something so physically demanding. I felt so relieved, so happy. My sunglasses were fogging up with tears. I couldn't hold back my emotions.

"Simon, I'm so emotional. I'm crying. Thank you, thank you!"

"You're welcome," he told me. "This is why I do this."

We gathered around the sign and took several photographs as a group. Then, I took several photos of signs, including one for my Papi's upcoming ninetieth birthday. We had been on Uhuru about fifteen minutes, and it was time to leave. It's not good for humans to be at that altitude for very long.

Besides, we still had to make our descent—and I had to throw up and use the bathroom again. I was so ready to get off the mountain. We had planned to do it in one day, instead of the typical two or three days, but my body had other ideas.

We started by jogging down the mountain, seesawing through the rocks and sliding through scree, the loose rock debris covering the ground. I'd have to stop, gag, and throw up, go to the restroom, and rest for a while. Then, I'd feel better and start jogging again. It became a vicious roller coaster, in which I would feel okay and then not so great.

By then, because of my stomach bug and altitude sickness, Martina was convinced I was dehydrated. I couldn't keep liquids down. My oxygen level was only 86 percent, which wasn't good. She knew I had to get off the mountain. She decided to stop giving me fluids because I just kept throwing up, which made me more dehydrated. We didn't bring an IV bag, which would have come in handy. When the antibiotics finally kicked in, I felt better and could eat something.

Rescues on Kili are never easy and are quite dangerous. We learned that firsthand when we encountered a woman who was lying on her side alone. She had fallen, only four hundred feet from the summit, and had broken her leg and dislocated her shoulder. Her guide and the rest of her group had left her alone, promising to come back for her. Simon shook his head and decided to stay with her. He called the closest camp and told them about the situation. He would have to carry her down because a helicopter couldn't reach that altitude.

I was still woozy, and Martina advised Ladi that we were going to stop at Mweka Camp, at about 10,138 feet. It was only midday, and I was exhausted from the stomach pain, nausea, dehydration, and altitude sickness. I'd never felt so miserable—and I've obviously felt bad before. Martina and I decided against a treatment, which would dehydrate me even more, and she gave me electrolytes instead. I slept through the night, throwing up now and then.

The next morning, I heard a helicopter flying overhead to rescue the injured woman. Ladi knocked on my tent and told me to get up. The porters brought us hot water to wash our dust-covered faces. I managed to eat two tiny bananas and part of an egg for breakfast.

That day, while descending the final five thousand feet to Mweka Gate, I probably had to stop at least two dozen times to take care of business. Eventually, nothing was left in my system. I didn't have much strength and was wobbly, but I made it down on my own. I called my parents and told them I was safe.

We walked another mile to Simon's family farm. It was near the park border, and he fed us a wonderful meal of farm-fresh food. I managed to eat only a banana and meat-filled pastry. There was a ceremony to say good-bye

It is not the mountain we conquer, but ourselves.

to the guides, cooks, and porters, and they sang and danced for us. Simon gave us a certificate confirming that we had reached Kili's summit.

As I reflect on reaching Kili's summit more than five years ago, I'm reminded of two famous quotes. The first is from Sir Edmund Hillary, the New Zealand mountaineer and explorer, who once said, "It is not the mountain we conquer, but ourselves." Hillary was one of the first two men to reach the summit of Mount Everest on May 29, 1953. The second is from David McCullough Jr., a noted American author and educator, who noted,

"Climb the mountain so you can see the world, not so the world can see you."

Reaching Kili's summit was the fulfillment of one of my lifelong goals, a resounding affirmation that I could accomplish anything despite my medical struggles. As we flew back to the US a couple of days later, I dreamt about the adventures that lay ahead. The sense of accomplishment was overpowering, along with immense gratitude toward Ladi, Martina, Simon, and the entire team that propelled me to the summit. I know I have never felt closer to God—both physically and spiritually—than I did in those brief moments on the summit. It was a connection with Him that left me longing for more, unaware at the time that my body had other plans.

CHAPTER SIXTEEN

STAY RESILIENT

As I begin the second quarter of my life, God is still throwing me curveballs. He must think there's a hole in my swing! The ongoing battle with symptoms of VATER, or VACTERAL syndrome, as it's commonly known now, is still a part of my journey. This includes the continual management of bowel control and addressing bone abnormalities, which contribute to my discomfort.

Adding to the expected challenges, I also learned that, for the third time in my life, I have a tethered spinal cord. Thankfully, I have reached a point in my life where I've stopped growing, so my spinal cord isn't under too much tension. Though my back will get stiff, and I sometimes feel a tingling or electric-like current from my thigh to my heel. For the most part, as long as

I keep moving, stretching, and exercising, I can manage the problem well.

In the spring of 2020, I received a diagnosis that changed my outlook on my health. I was showing signs of Klippel-Feil syndrome (KFS), a rare condition that impacts the development of the bones in my spine. According to the National Institute of Health (NIH), people with KFS are born with "abnormal fusion of at least two spinal bones (vertebrae) in the neck. Common features may include a short neck, low hairline at the back of the head, and restricted movement of the upper spine." Some people with KFS have no symptoms. Others may have frequent headaches, back and neck pain, and other nerve issues. Even worse: people with KFS are at risk for severe spinal injury. Astonishingly, the NIH estimates that one in forty thousand people have KFS, and wouldn't you know it? I find myself among them.

After I was first diagnosed with KFS, I didn't notice any symptoms. Over time, however, it became more difficult for me to turn my head without discomfort, like when I'm looking both ways while driving. My neck is sometimes stiff and sore. I crack my neck to make it feel better.

However, in the fall of 2023, my symptoms and discomfort became more severe. One morning at the gym, I was doing crunches, a seemingly easy exercise, and I felt searing pain that locked up my neck. In November, while I was visiting my grandmother in the hospital after she had back surgery, my mother noticed that I couldn't get comfortable while sitting in a chair. Mom told my grandmother's neurosurgeon about it, and he ordered an MRI for me.

A couple of weeks later, we went back to get the results of the MRI. I'll be honest: I didn't want to go to the doctor that day. I had a pit in my stomach because I knew he was going to deliver bad news. People tried

I had a pit in my stomach because I knew he was going to deliver bad news.

to encourage me by telling me it was just sore muscles, but I knew it was probably something serious given my medical history.

When the doctor showed me the MRI results, he explained that my C4 and C5 and C6 and C7 vertebrae had fused together. That was the reason I had a stiff neck. As the doctor looked at the MRI, he kept saying, "This is really strange. This is really strange."

"Just be careful," the doctor told me. "Don't worry too much about it because, believe it or not, your body is healing itself. The good news is that I won't have to go in to do a fusion."

Overall, the doctor's words brought me a sense of relief. A stiff neck seemed like a small price to pay after a lifetime of discomfort. I wasn't going to need another surgery and wasn't in danger of not being able to walk. It turned out to be good news in the end.

However, just as Mom and I were preparing to leave the office, the doctor dropped some unexpected news that hit me like a colossal hammer: "You know, JT, your outdoor activities and adventures are going to have to slow down. You're going to have to be more careful."

The realization that I could no longer indulge in what I loved most almost felt like a life-altering sentence. The outdoors, with all its adventures, is not just a hobby for me; it's truly a way of life. It's where I discover my identity and find fulfillment. Climbing majestic mountains, winding down the slopes of the Rockies on skis, racing mountain bikes on challenging Colorado trails, running along the breathtaking rim of the Grand Canyon—each outdoor adventure brings me unparalleled joy and elation, surpassing any other experience I've had. In the outdoors I find peace and serenity, form meaningful bonds with others, and connect with God in ways that I can't elsewhere. Most importantly, it's through these adventures that I raise money for my foundation that benefits so many worthy causes. Being told to scale back on these pursuits was completely unexpected.

After hearing that somber prognosis from the doctor, the weight of it all kept me home from work for two days. It was during the holidays, but I wasn't in a very festive mood. Attending a friend's wedding in Florida offered a diversion, but my mind was elsewhere. The four-hour drive to my grandmother's house in Florida with my parents, normally chatty, was unusually quiet. No one wanted to address the proverbial elephant in the room.

Little changed once we reached my grandmother's house. I was unusually tired and slept late, seemingly unable to get out of my funk. To lift my spirits, Dad tried to talk me into playing a game of pickleball. Reluctant at first, I begrudgingly decided to go. After the match, I thanked him for getting me out of my comfort zone. However, when he responded with a sarcastic remark, my frustration erupted. I rarely raise my voice at anyone, let alone my parents.

"Nobody understands what I'm going through!" I exclaimed. "You don't have to go through the pain every day. The adventures are what I live for, and it's how I raise money."

Following the Christmas holiday, we flew to Colorado, which proved to be an uncomfortable trip. I couldn't sit in my seat on the plane, as the nerve pain was so bad that my arm went numb if I sat for too long. I was forced to walk up and down the aisle. Once in Colorado,

I visited the comforting hands of my favorite massage therapist, a familiar support in times of need.

"We're going to get through this," she said. "I have a lot of great ideas to give you comfort and hopefully change some things in your body."

After New Year's Day, I was able to get an appointment with Dr. Sonny Gill, an orthopedic spine surgeon at the Steadman Clinic in Vail, Colorado. Dr. Gill looked

Dr. Gill gave me hope that my life wouldn't have to change so dramatically.

at my MRI and immediately gave me a much more positive outlook.

"My job is to get your life back to what you're used to," Dr. Gill said. "I've worked with a professional skier who had the same condition and he's back racing. We won't have to do surgery now, but we might have to do it down the road. I'm going to do everything I can to make sure you can do everything that you want."

As Dr. Gill told me the good news, he placed his hand on my knee. I had tears in my eyes, as I was overwhelmed with joy. Dr. Gill gave me hope that my life wouldn't have to change so dramatically. Sure, there would be some tough days in physical therapy, but it was better than the alternative.

The next day, I had a videoconference with another surgeon from the Johns Hopkins Hospital in Baltimore, Maryland. Thankfully, his opinion was similar to Dr. Gill's in that I could remain active, although the second surgeon advised me to be a little more careful with no running or high-impact sports. He didn't say I had to completely shut it down either. I changed my diet and eliminated foods that cause inflammation. I felt better in only a couple of weeks. I've even fasted at times to help.

One of the primary reasons I was so anxious about being diagnosed with Klippel-Feil syndrome is that I jumped on the Internet to find out everything I could about the rare condition. I watched YouTube and TikTok videos of people describing their scary symptoms. Some of them were in agonizing pain and couldn't run or exercise. The future seemed bleak.

However, there was one story that inspired me. Justyn Ross of Phenix City, Alabama, was one of the best high school football players in the country when he signed with Clemson University in 2018. He was one of the Tigers' most important players as a freshman, catching forty-six passes for one thousand yards with nine touchdowns.

In the College Football Playoff National Championship against No. 1–ranked Alabama on January 7, 2019, Ross caught six passes for 153 yards. He hauled in a seventy-four-yard touchdown pass from quarterback Trevor Lawrence in the third quarter of a 44–16 victory. Analysts projected that if freshmen were eligible to be selected in the National Football League, Ross would have been a first-round pick in the 2019 NFL Draft. He was that good. Ross was just as explosive as a sophomore with sixty-six catches for 865 yards with eight touchdowns in 2019.

Then, just like that, football was nearly taken away from him.

In the spring of 2020, Ross was tackled by a teammate in practice. He felt numbness and tingling in his arms. He figured it was another stinger, which is a common injury in football. Doctors put him through a battery of tests, and he felt good enough to go back to practice a few days later. However, Tigers coach Dabo Swinney called him to his office. There were a lot of doctors in the room, and Ross's mother was listening to the conversation through a speakerphone.

Doctors delivered the devastating news: Ross had been born with KFS and might never play football again. It was the first time an MRI had been taken of his neck. He was stunned. Against doctors' wishes, Ross was determined to keep playing. Ross and his mother found a surgeon in Pittsburgh, Pennsylvania, who believed he could relieve the pressure on his spine, making it safe for him to play football again. He had surgery in June 2020. Ross missed the following season to spend time strengthening the muscles supporting his neck and spine.

Against all odds, Ross returned to the field in 2021. He caught forty-six passes for 514 yards with three touchdowns in ten games. A left foot injury sidelined him for the final three games. Because of concerns about his neck injury, NFL teams passed on selecting Ross in the 2022 draft. The Kansas City Chiefs signed him as a free agent. Ross missed the 2022 season after undergoing foot surgery, but he made the active roster the next year. He was the first player with KFS ever cleared by doctors to compete in the NFL. Ross's prayers were answered.

I know one thing: I had an army of prayer warriors behind me, and their prayers were beginning to be answered. I truly believe that Satan can enter our lives during tough times and try to take advantage of us when we're having doubts. During those most difficult times, we must turn to God for guidance. He has a plan for all of us. We just must be still and listen. In the Bible, Jeremiah implored the people of Judah to listen to God's message, to pay attention, and to obey. He warned them to honor God before it was too late: "Give glory to the LORD your God before He causes darkness, and before your feet stumble on the dark mountains, and while you are looking for light, He turns it into the shadow of death and makes it dense darkness" (Jeremiah 13:16 NKJV).

In some ways, I walked in the shadow of death during my latest health scare and felt as if my life was over. At times, it did feel like I was climbing a mountain in darkness. However, after the promising prognosis I received from the surgeons, I walked out of the shadow. I'm walking with God very closely again. I'm still not exactly sure what the future holds. I'm not completely out of the woods yet with my neck. I know one thing: I'll keep climbing with a smile on my face.

Put one foot in front of the other. Endure and prevail. Maintain your resilience and continue your ascent.

That's the final message I hope to leave you with. No matter the circumstances—whether you're fifty yards from the summit of Mount Kilimanjaro, halfway to the finish line in your first marathon, deep into an all-night study session for a final exam, or just down in the dumps because everything seems to be going against you—keep pushing forward. Put one foot in front of the other. Endure and prevail. Maintain your resilience and continue your ascent.

In my short time on earth, the Lord knows the extent of my endurance. Whether it was grappling with a laundry list of medical issues, overcoming learning differences, or facing seemingly insurmountable challenges in the great outdoors, I've sought to embody unwavering strength and spirit. I've learned to bounce back from setbacks and be adaptable. Hopefully, with each trial, I've not only endured but also learned and grown. I'll always know one thing: There are no bad days—only hard ones.

ACKNOWLEDGMENTS

THANK YOU TO MY LORD AND SAVIOR, JESUS Christ, who has healed me so many times and has given me the strength and courage to get up again. I know I wouldn't be where I am today without my steadfast faith.

Thank you to my parents, Jim and Kristine Mestdagh, who stood up for me when I wasn't old enough or strong enough to do it myself, and for teaching me never to let my differences or any obstacle stand in the way of accomplishing everything God has envisioned for me.

Thank you to my grandparents, my late Papi, my Nani, Pa, and my late Ma, for loving me, encouraging me, and supporting me throughout my life.

Thank you to my mentors, friends, doctors, tutors, and teachers, so many of whom are named in this book. Without your friendship, guidance, patience, and kindness, none of this would have been possible.

ACKNOWLEDGMENTS

Thank you so much to Anita Palmer, Lesley Burbridge, Greg Lucid, and the team at Forefront Books for believing in me and allowing me to share my story of encouragement. I hope it changes a few lives along the way.

A tremendous thank-you to Mark Schlabach for putting my thoughts and words into a story that I pray touches lives!

NOTES

1 “Kilimanjaro - Umbwe Route - 7 Days.” HolyFisher Tours. Accessed February 1, 2024. https://holyfisher.com/shop/kiliumb-wwb7-kilimanjaro-umbwe-route-7-days-188#attr=.

2 Admin. “Pole Pole! Go Slow and Connect.” Tanzania adventures (Safari, Kilimanjaro trek, Eco-adventures), March 21, 2019. https://www.nomadicexperience.com/slowtravel/#:~:text=Pole%20pole%20is%20also%20the,you%20are%20here%20and%20now.

3 Emily Perl Kingsley, “Welcome to Holland,” 1987. Reprinted with author’s permission.

4 Dawn@cedarsstory.com. “Welcome to Holland Interview with Emily Perl Kingsley.” Cedars Story, November 5, 2019. https://www.cedarsstory.com/welcome-holland-interview-author-emily-perl-kingsley/.

5 Manry, Kaitlin. “Sacia’s Promise: Marysville Student’s Drive for College and a Better Future.” HeraldNet.com, September 11, 2010. https://www.heraldnet.com/news/sacias-promise-marysville-students-drive-for-college-and-a-better-future/.

6 Ibid.

7 Ibid.

8 Ibid.

9 Ibid.

10 Misner, Ivan. "Change Your Words, Inspire Your World...: Dr. Ivan Misner®." Dr. Ivan Misner® | Business Networking, November 26, 2017. https://ivanmisner.com/change-words-inspire-world/.

11 Edenloff, Celeste. "John Smith of 'breakthrough' Shares Story of near Drowning." Alexandria Echo Press, February 24, 2020. https://www.echopress.com/community/john-smith-of-breakthrough-shares-story-of-near-drowning.

12 Ibid.

13 Ibid.

14 Salvador, Joseph. "ESPN's Dan Orlovsky Says Prayer for Damar Hamlin during 'NFL Live ..." Sports Illustrated, January 4, 2023. https://www.si.com/nfl/2023/01/04/espn-dan-orlovsky-says-prayer-for-damar-hamlin-during-nfl-live.

15 Getzenberg, Alaina. "Damar Hamlin on First Padded Practice Back: 'It Feels Amazing.'" ESPN, July 31, 2023. https://www.espn.com/nfl/story/_/id/38109474/damar-hamlin-first-padded-practice-back-feels-amazing.

16 Dragon, Tyler. "Buffalo Bills' Damar Hamlin Makes Surprise Appearance at NFL Honors Awards Show." USA Today, February 10, 2023. https://www.usatoday.com/story/sports/nfl/2023/02/09/damar-hamlin-hits-nfl-honors-stage-surprise-appearance-show/11225071002/.

17 Baron, Zach. "How Chance the Rapper's Life Became Perfect." GQ, August 24, 2016. https://www.gq.com/story/how-chance-the-rappers-life-became-perfect.

18 Bonaguro, Alison. "Chance the Rapper on Achieving Goals as an Independent Artist & Paying It Forward." SUCCESS, August 10, 2023. https://www.success.com/chance-the-rapper/.

19 Peña, A. *Monologues of a Pediatric Surgeon*. United States: A. Peña, 2011.

20 Mestdagh, JT. Interview with Darius Ziabakhsh. Personal, August 9, 2023.

21 Ibid.

22 Media, ASH. "New Surgeon General Advisory Raises Alarm about the Devastating Impact of the Epidemic of Loneliness and Isolation in the United States." HHS.gov, May 3, 2023. https://www.hhs.gov/about/news/2023/05/03/new-surgeon-general-advisory-raises-alarm-about-devastating-impact-epidemic-loneliness-isolation-united-states.html.

23 Ibid.

24 Stanton, Andrew, and Angus MacLane. 2016. *Finding Dory*. United States: Walt Disney Studios Motion Pictures.

25 1. "Dyslexia Basics," International Dyslexia Association, March 10, 2020, https://dyslexiaida.org/dyslexia-basics/.

26 ..."...Until Everyone Can Read!" International Dyslexia Association. Accessed February 1, 2024. https://dyslexiaida.org/..

27 Costello, Brian. "Dyslexia Could Never Sack Tebow." New York Post, August 3, 2012. https://nypost.com/2012/08/03/dyslexia-could-never-sack-tebow/.

28 Ibid.

29 Mestdagh, JT. Interview with Kes Tomlin. Personal, October 6, 2023.

30 JT Mestdagh, Interview with Kes Tomlin, personal, October 6, 2023.

31 Jamal, Azim, and Nido R. Qubein. *Life balance: The sufi way*. Mumbai, India: Jaico Pub. House, 2007.

32 Mestdagh, JT. Interview with Matthew Olson. Personal, July 7, 2023.

33 Bowman, Alisa. "Social Media's Effects on the Teen Brain." Mayo Clinic, September 8, 2023. https://mcpress.mayoclinic.org/parenting/social-media-affects-teens-brains/.

34 Ibid.

35 Mestdagh, JT. Interview with Chris R. Mazzarella. Personal, August 9, 2023.

36 Duffey, Clare. "Many US Teens 'Almost Constantly' Using YouTube, Tiktok, New Pew ..." CNN.com, December 11, 2023.

https://edition.cnn.com/2023/12/11/tech/teens-youtube-tik-tok-pew-research/index.html.

37 Visé, Daniel de. "Teens Are Spending Less Time than Ever with Friends." Yahoo!, June 7, 2023. https://www.yahoo.com/lifestyle/teens-spending-less-time-ever-100000737.html.

38 Kartvedt, Scott. *Full Throttle: From the Blue Angels to Hollywood Stunt Pilot*. New York, NY: HIgh Performance Climb, 2023.

39 Mestdagh, JT. Interview with Scott Kartvedt. Other, August 15, 2023.

40 Goldberg, Dan, Jon Lucas, and Scott Moore. *The hangover*. United States: Warner Bros., 2009.

41 Graham, Kendra. "'I'm Making Pearls in Here!'" Decision Magazine, October 11, 2018. https://decisionmagazine.com/im-making-pearls-here/.

42 Ibid.

43 Sweatt, Lydia. "11 Quotes about Leaving a Legacy." SUCCESS, July 31, 2018. https://www.success.com/11-quotes-about-leaving-a-legacy/.

44 Staff. "21 of Maya Angelou's Best Quotes to Inspire ." Harper's Bazaar, May 22, 2017. https://www.harpersbazaar.com/culture/features/a9874244/best-maya-angelou-quotes/.

45 Staff. "Beautifully Flawed Foundation." Beautifully Flawed Foundation, December 20, 2023. https://beautifullyflawedfoundation.com/.

46 Carr, Madeleine. "How Professional Surfer Bethany Hamilton Is Doing It All." Hawaii Magazine, January 21, 2021. https://www.hawaiimagazine.com/how-professional-surfer-bethany-hamilton-is-doing-it-all/.

47 Ibid.

48 Mestdagh, JT. Interview with Lily Wright. Personal, May 20, 2023.

ABOUT THE AUTHOR

JT Mestdagh is a young entrepreneur, philanthropist, podcaster, and inspirational speaker based in Grosse Pointe, Michigan. A graduate of High Point University in North Carolina, JT is also an experienced mountaineer, extreme skier, boater, hunter, and adventurer who has made it his life mission to encourage people to untether from natural or self-imposed limitations and live full, passionate lives.

Born with life-threatening VATER/VACTERL syndrome, as well as extreme dyslexia and short-term memory loss, he established the JT Mestdagh Foundation to bring encouragement, joy, and laughter to people with physical and learning disabilities and to their families. JT hopes that through his life experiences and other people's stories, the reader is reminded there truly are no bad days and to never give up.

MISSION

The JT Mestdagh Foundation believes in making a difference in the world by lifting up children with congenital colorectal issues, ensuring they get world-class medical care. We're also here for kids with dyslexia and other learning differences, helping them thrive with top-notch educational testing, mentoring, and tutoring—especially through the Tattum Reading program. And it's not just about the kids; we're all about supporting their families, caregivers, and educators too, with love, hope, and real tools to make life a little easier. Because no one should have to face these challenges alone. By reaching up and reaching out, a world is changed and improved.

For more information about the foundation and how you can help, go to JTMestdaghFoundation.org

JOURNAL PROMPTS FOR *NO BAD DAYS*

Chapter 1: What is on your bucket list? What's on your list that takes you out of your comfort zone?

Chapter 2: What is your story?

Chapter 3: What friends could you pray for today?

Chapter 4: How can you inspire others with positivity?

Chapter 5: Who can you be a better friend to this week? What things could you do for that person?

Chapter 6: What are some of your favorite memories with your friends? With your family?

Chapter 7: How can you be more authentic in your actions and behavior?

Chapter 8: What are three good labels you could use to describe yourself?

Chapter 9: What are three ways you could stretch yourself in the next six months?

Chapter 10: Can you think of a moment when you had to put yourself in someone else's shoes?

Chapter 11: Try spending a day "unplugged" from social media. How did it make you feel? Were you more productive? Were you more connected with your friends and family?

Chapter 12: Think of a time when you learned how to fall. What lessons did you learn?

Chapter 13: Who is your wolf pack? What ways could you help each other grow?

Chapter 14: What kind of a legacy do you want to leave?

Chapter 15: What's something you're proud of yourself for accomplishing? What was the journey like to get there?

Chapter 16: What is something you've learned in the last week? In the last month? In the last year? What can you do to continue learning?